D0368981

DATE DUE
5 3 10

Off to a Good Start

Off

464 Readiness Activities for Reading, Math, Social Studies, and Science

to a Good Start

AMY L. TOOLE and ELLEN BOEHM
Illustrations by Nancy Shufelt

WALKER AND COMPANY, NEW YORK

First published in the United States of America in 1983 by the Walker Publishing Company, Inc.
Published simultaneously in Canada by John Wiley & Sons Canada, Limited, Rexdale, Ontario.
ISBN: 0-8027-9179-4
Book design by Laura Ferguson
Library of Congress Catalog Card Number: 82-13474
Printed in the United States of America
10 9 8 7 6 5 4 3 2 1

Library of Congress Cataloging in Publication Data

Toole, Amy L.
Off to a good start.
Bibliography: p.
1. Readiness for school. 2. Reading readiness.
3. Mathematics—Study and teaching (Preschool)
4. Social sciences—Study and teaching (Preschool)
5. Science—Study and teaching (Preschool) I. Boehm, Ellen. II. Title.
LB1132.T66 1983 372'.21 82-13474
ISBN 0-8027-9179-4

This work was developed under the auspices of the Putnam/Northern Westchester Board of Cooperative Educational Services (BOCES), Department of Special Education, Yorktown Heights, New York. However, the content does not necessarily reflect the position or policy of BOCES; no official endorsement of these materials should be inferred.

BOCES Series Editor: Kenn Goin
Illustrator: Nancy Shufelt

ACKNOWLEDGMENTS

We wish to thank the Board of Cooperative Educational Services for supporting the development of this book. Special thanks are given to Dr. Paul Irvine, Director of Special Education, and Dr. Donald Coe, Assistant Director of Special Education, for encouraging the development of these readiness activities. We are in the debt of Mr. James Rieger, Principal of Thomas Jefferson School in the Lakeland Public School District, Yorktown Heights, New York, for providing a warm and caring setting for field testing the activities.

Amy L. Toole
Ellen Boehm

Contents

Preface

Some children enter kindergarten with fewer skills than their peers. These youngsters, even though they may have come from a preschool, often are unready for the methods of learning used in kindergarten. This curriculum offers activities that revolve around *play*—the basic learning mode of preschool. Yet, the activities teach the same skills that many kindergartners learn through traditional classroom methods.

The Children

These activities are well-suited to kindergarten-age children who are a little behind their peers. These children are often "placed" in special programs with six- and seven-year-olds or in preschools with younger children. But they may do very well if their kindergarten teacher has an array of activities at her disposal that can address their learning needs as well as those of their peers.

The readiness games in this book emphasize play, concrete experiences, and tasks broken into very small learning steps. They allow slower children to catch up to their peers while remaining in the most appropriate learning setting for their age—kindergarten.

But the book also provides sound experiences for normally progressing youngsters in kindergarten. It is a perfect supplement to the teacher's armory of traditional kindergarten activities—or it may be used as the basis for a complete program.

Specifically, the activities in the book are designed to be used by:

- youngsters who are attending a special or regular nursery school and who are preparing for kindergarten entry;
- children who have had no nursery school experiences prior to entering kindergarten and who, therefore, may be behind others in their class in skills development;
- five-year-olds, delayed by one or two years in one or more skills areas, who are enrolled in kindergarten;
- children who are determined "not ready" for school after kindergar-

ten screenings and are asked to stay home from school for an additional year; and

- regular kindergartners

Developing the Book

The various activities in this book were devised on the basis of certain premises regarding learning and development.

First, children need a firm foundation in the basic developmental areas—language, cognition, motor development, social/emotional development, and self-help. While the curriculum is not organized around these areas, it is designed to develop the child's skills in communication, thinking, movement, relating to others, and taking care of his own needs.

Second, all children pass through a number of stages in learning. Although the rate of movement through these stages may vary, the stages are sequential. If a child does not complete learning at one stage, he* will have trouble moving to the next stage. The activities in this book are carefully organized so that the early activities in each chapter develop abilities needed for the later activities in that chapter. The teacher always must be aware of the student's readiness to engage in particular activities before beginning them.

Third, youngsters who are developmentally behind need extra help to catch up. The earlier the help is given, the better chance the child has to move up with his peers. For this reason, a number of very basic activities that many children can do by the time they enter kindergarten (e.g., "saying their own names") are included in this curriculum.

Fourth, children learn best through concrete experiences. This book provides those experiences in every area, but most notably in the areas of science and social studies, where concepts are often beyond the reach of the young child unless they are supported with visual, tactile, and auditory activities.

Fifth, children can make progress best when all instruction is geared to achieve certain goals. The activities in this book are designed:

a) to prepare children for academic work; and

b) to motivate children to learn.

*To avoid the distraction of "he or she," "s/he," and other variations, the pronoun "he" is used throughout when referring to students. No bias is intended; it is a matter of convenience only.

The second goal—learning motivation—is achieved by teaching through play rather than primarily through written or sit-down tasks, teaching by breaking each activity into small, easily accomplished steps, and capitalizing on the child's curiosity and his love of imitation and exploration.

These premises, along with developmental checklists that provide types of behaviors children normally exhibit by certain ages fully considered in structuring the activities—particularly those for reading and math.

Once the activities were compiled, they were used in a transitional kindergarten classroom at Thomas Jefferson Elementary School (Yorktown Heights, N.Y.) on a regular basis. Test results for the 1981-82 school year indicated statistically significant cognitive gains for the class. The *McCarthy Scales of Children's Abilities,* a widely known standardized test, was used for pre- and post-assessment.

The Curriculum's Structure

The activities in this volume fall into four chapters:

Chapter 1 Reading and General Readiness
Chapter 2 Math Readiness
Chapter 3 Social Studies Readiness
Chapter 4 Science Readiness

Chapters 1 and 2 are organized by objectives that each child should complete in the sequence presented. A specific set of activities is provided for each objective.

Chapters 3 and 4 are organized by units. The whole group of children should be taken through each unit together since most four- and five-year-old children have little knowledge of these areas and need to learn all of the concepts presented.

Within each objective or unit, the level of activities moves from easy to somewhat more difficult. Consequently, the activities should be conducted in sequence unless the teacher is using *Off to a Good Start* as a supplement to other materials.

How to Schedule the Activities

In general, each chapter has more than enough activities for a year's instruction in that area. The reading and math readiness chapters have enough activities for the teacher to present three or four new ones each week, if desired. The social studies and science chapters each have nine major units, which can be used at a rate of one per month if appropriate. Social studies contains a tenth unit on holidays which can be used throughout the year.

If the teacher is using this volume supplementally—that is, not as the primary curricular tool—it is necessary to ensure the child's readiness for each activity before beginning. This means the teacher must have a good sense of each child's level of "readiness." Readiness means not only the presence of requisite *knowledge* for the activity to be undertaken, but an *attention span* and a *social readiness* that meets the needs of the lesson. The teacher should not proceed with an activity until the child is ready for it.

Materials

Materials needed are listed at the beginning of each activity. They should be on hand before starting the lesson. The experienced teacher should feel free to substitute materials as necessary, so long as they serve the same end as the original items. It is important to choose materials that are safe, durable, and as inexpensive as the market allows.

Grouping

In general, social studies and science should be taught to all the children at the same time. Items in reading and math, however, should be presented in small groups or individually, for children come into programs with differing levels of skill in these areas. Grouping should always be flexible since children move at different speeds.

Staffing Needs

The activities are designed for teachers, paraprofessionals, and parents. Generally, the teacher should teach the activity first. Then, if individual instruction appears appropriate for some of the children, a teacher's aide or parent volunteer can spend more time with those students in helping them to master the activity.

CHAPTER 1

Reading and General Readiness

OBJECTIVES IN CHAPTER 1

We often take for granted that five-year-olds can tell us their names. We are sometimes wrong. Some youngsters in this age group have as much trouble responding to the question, "What is your full name?" as they do to the question, "What is the first letter of the alphabet?"

The kind of information and skills we often assume to be acquired by five-year-olds is the domain of this chapter. We have found frequently that children who were not ready for kindergarten were not ready precisely because they did not have very basic *general* knowledge. This material is crucial for getting ready to learn to read or to understand quantitative concepts—in short, for academic work in general.

In this chapter we offer 123 activities to help prepare children for the first steps into academic work. The activities are organized under fifteen objectives, which move from relatively easy tasks to relatively more complex undertakings.

The activities provide fun and interesting ways to learn the objectives. Though these activities may become a part of your daily routine, they should always be approached in a game-like manner. All children learn best when they succeed often and fail rarely. To help the children succeed, you should: (1) break learning into small steps; (2) avoid frustration by not going beyond children's attention spans; (3) review often; and (4) reward (orally) frequently.

Be sure children have the necessary skills and knowledge to engage in an activity before you introduce it. Know their strengths and weaknesses. In some cases it may be necessary to help a child individually before he can work successfully with a group on an activity.

Most of these activities are designed for both group and individual work. Use your own discretion in deciding which approach would be most effective with your students. Only Objective 15, which introduces more advanced material, has activities designed exclusively for group work.

OBJECTIVE 1

RECITES OWN NAME

Objective: Children will recite their own first and last names when asked.

Before beginning, explain: Each person has a name given to him when he is born. It is important that all people know their names and are able to tell them to other people. The game we are going to play helps us see how names are important.

A. POLICEMAN

Materials: policeman's hat (optional) and policeman's badge (optional)

1. Assign one child the role of policeman.
2. Tell all children: "Everybody stand up. Give your full name to the policeman when he asks. If you give your full name, you can sit down. You can't sit down unless you give your full name." Assure the children that everyone will have a turn as policeman during the coming days.
3. Then, prompt the policeman to ask each child: "Who are you?" or "What is your name?"
4. When each child has been asked for a name, you should then take over and say to those children still standing: "Everyone can sit down now." Then encourage those children by saying, for example: "Sandy, you know your name. Say it with me. 'Sandy Dunn.' Good."
5. You may repeat the game or wait until a day or two passes.

OBJECTIVE 2

RECOGNIZES OWN WRITTEN NAME

Objective: Children will recognize their names by sight.

Before beginning, explain: Every person's name can be written as well as spoken. I use the written names when I mark who is present and absent. The games we are going to play help us know how our names look.

A. I'M HERE

Materials: index cards (1 per pupil) and pen or felt marker

1. Write each class member's first and last names on an index card.
2. Have the cards stacked blank side up. Each morning, ask the children to gather around you, and then turn the cards up, one at a time.
3. As each name appears, the child to whom it belongs must raise a hand or say "Here." Give the children their name cards whenever they respond correctly. For a while you may have to simply show the children their names and read them aloud until they have seen the names enough to recognize them. (You may make the cards more attractive with borders, colored ink, or foil stars.)
4. This procedure can be repeated each morning for attendance. Simply be sure to collect the cards at the end of the activity.

B. CLOTHESPIN ATTENDANCE

Materials: metal coffee can and clothespins (1 per pupil)

1. Collect a metal can (be careful of sharp edges) and enough spring-type clothespins for each student in your class. Write a class member's name on each pin. Use initials for the last names if there is not enough room on the pin.
2. Place all the pins on a table and ask each child, in turn, to pick out the clothespin with his name on it and to place it on the rim of the can.
3. Once the children are familiar with the task (and can recognize their names) you can have them pick out their names each morning as they come in. This routine will take care of attendance.

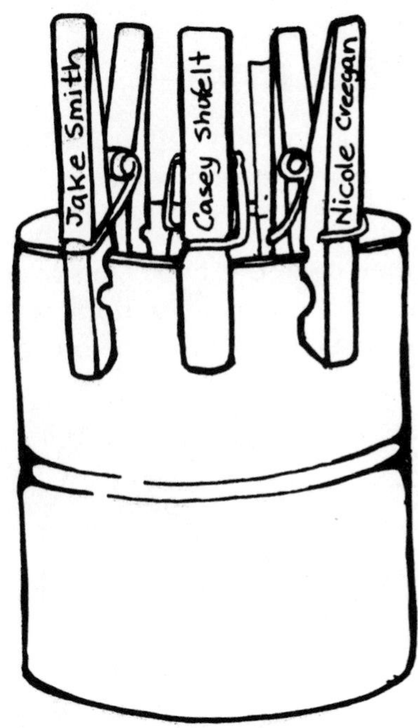

OBJECTIVE 3

RECITES OWN ADDRESS

Objective: Children will recite their addresses without help.

Before beginning, explain: Each person in this class lives in a different house from all the other people in the class (note: except brothers or sisters in the same class). Each of our homes has its own *address*. An address says where the home is—for example, what street it's on. Any mail we or our families get is sent to our address. The game we are going to play helps us learn our own address.

A. WHERE I LIVE

Materials: construction paper (2 different colors per child); marker; scissors; bulletin board

1. Make enough houses (or apartment buildings) for all children to have their own. Use two colors of construction paper and make the roofs one color and the rest of the structures another. Write a child's full name on each roof.

2. Show each child his house. Say: "See, your name is on it." Then say: "Can you tell me your address?" If there is no response, say the address for the child. Then say: "Now you say it."

3. When the child can recite the address, place the house on the bulletin board.

OBJECTIVE 4

RECITES OWN PHONE NUMBER

Objective: Children will recite their phone numbers without help.

Before beginning, explain: Each phone has a different number. For example, my phone's number is 768–9312. Your phone number is very important to learn because you may need to tell it to someone if you have trouble or get lost. The game we are going to play shows who knows their number and helps those who do not to learn theirs.

A. HELLO, NUMBER PLEASE?

Materials: construction paper phones (1 per child) and bulletin board

1. Make a phone of construction paper for each child. On each phone's dial, place a child's name and telephone number.
2. Determine which children know their phone numbers by asking each individual: "What is your telephone number?" Those children who can answer should have their paper phones posted next to their houses on the board.
3. Each day, work on phone numbers with all children, but especially with those who have not been able to recite theirs to you. Say to each child: "Here is your telephone number. It is 768–1245. Now say it with me as I point to each number—768–1245. Good. Now you try to say it without me." If the child can still not repeat the number, have him say it one more time with you, then leave the task until the next class. Always encourage the child—even if the number has not been learned—by saying: "That's good. You almost have it."

OBJECTIVE 5

LEFT-TO-RIGHT PROGRESSION

Objective: The child will learn to go from left to right (left-to-right progression).

Before beginning, explain: Most of you use your right hand more than your left. Pick up a crayon—which hand is it in? If it's in your left, that's fine, but most people would have used their other hand. When people write or read, their hands or eyes move across the page in one direction. See (demonstrate). My hand moves from this side of the page (or blackboard), which is *left,* to this side, which is *right.* The games we will play today help us learn left and right and which way to move.

A. THE NAME GAME

Materials: colored picture cards (5)

1. Place a set of five picture cards in a row on a table before the child.
2. Then say: "Point to each card, starting on your left, and tell me what you see." (Child can name animal, color, etc.)
3. Repeat several times.

B. STRINGING ME ALONG

Materials: 2 identical sets of large beads (5 beads per set) and string

1. Prepare a sample. Put five different colored beads on a string.
2. Place the sample on a table so that it is horizontal to the child. Then give the child five duplicate beads. Say: "Repeat the pattern that you see here with these beads." You may

choose to have the child put the beads in correct order before stringing. Make sure he moves from left to right.

C. PEG PLAY

Materials: pegboard and pegs (8 pegs, 4 colors)

1. Start a two-color design on a pegboard. It may be one red peg followed by one blue peg.
2. Give the child two pegs and say: "Repeat my pattern with your pegs." The child may place the pattern under or to the side of your row. In either case, make sure the child goes from left to right.
3. If the child works well with the first easy design, go to three or four colors. If there is trouble with the first design, use only one color. The important concept at this point is left to right, not patterns.

D. CUBES

Materials: 10 cubes

1. Have two piles of one-inch cubes. Have the child sit at the table next to you and have one pile of cubes in front of him, one in front of you.
2. Make a left-to-right design. Ask the child: "Can you do this? Show me."
3. Make sure the child moves from left to right while working on repeating the design.

E. GIANT STEPS

1. This game may be played with an individual or group.
2. Ask the child to take different types of steps (i.e., big or little) either to the right or left.

3. As a variation, have one child be the leader. That child takes a right or left step. The other children repeat the step and say "Right" or "Left" as they take it. Be sure the leader is facing in the same direction as the other children.

F. SIMON SAYS

1. Play Simon Says with one child or a group.

2. Have Simon (you) stand next to the child and begin: "Simon says touch your left eye. Simon says touch your right ear." Continue with other left-right directions.

G. WORKSHEETS

Materials: worksheets (see example) and crayons

1. Prepare a worksheet with several horizontal rows of flowers, stars, squares, or other subjects. Hand out one worksheet to each child.

2. Ask the children to color the objects in each row. Make sure they understand to go from left to right across the page, doing one row at a time.

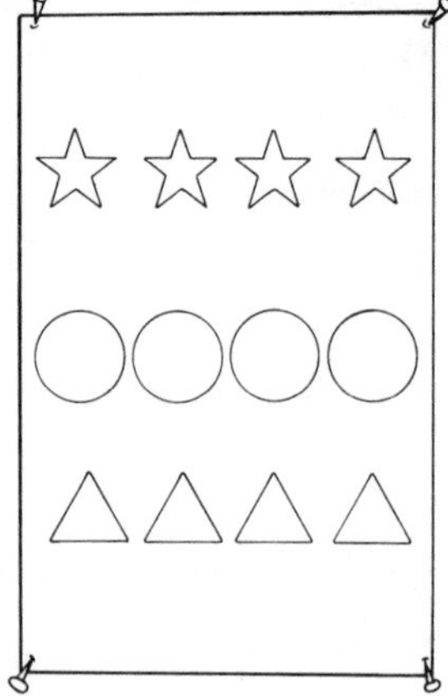

OBJECTIVE 6

UNDERSTANDS CONCEPTS OF SAME AND DIFFERENT

Objective: The child will tell whether objects are the same or different.

Before beginning, explain: There are two words we must know: *same, different.* If we say something is the same—like Susan's blond hair and John's blond hair—we mean it looks alike. If we say something is different—such as John's blond hair and Jim's black hair—we mean it does not look alike. The activities we'll do today help us to understand these words.

A. PICTURE CARD MATCHING

Materials: picture cards (2 sets of 5)

1. Use two sets of identical picture cards.
2. Place one set on the floor and hold the other in your hand.
3. Have the child sit on the floor and, as you show one card at a time from your hand, have the youngster pick one exactly like it from the cards on the floor. Stress the fact that the cards are the *same.*

B. CRAYON MATCHING

Materials: crayons (2 boxes)

1. Have ready two boxes of crayons. Give the child one of them.
2. From the remaining box, pick a crayon and say to the pupil: "Find one just the *same.*"

C. RELATIONSHIP SHAPES

Materials: 2 identical sets of shapes (geometric) or attribute blocks

1. Place a pile of shapes (or attribute blocks) on the table in front of the child.
2. Then, hold up a shape and ask the child: "Do you see one that is the *same*? Can you show me?"

D. CRAYONS AGAIN

Materials: 3 crayons (2 blue, 1 red)

1. Place two blue crayons and one red crayon on a table.
2. Ask the child to find the one that is *different* or *not the same.*

E. SHAPES AGAIN

Materials: 2 triangles and 1 circle

1. Place two triangles and one circle on a table.
2. Ask the child to find the one that is *different* or *not the same.*

F. PICTURE CARDS AGAIN

Materials: 3 picture cards (2 the same, 1 different)

1. Place two cards that are the same (identical) and one that is different on a table.
2. Ask the child to find the one that is *different* or *not the same.*

G. SOCKS AND SHOES

Materials: 3 dolls with socks

1. Have several dolls, each with a different pair of socks. Take one sock off each doll. Of these socks, hold up one to the child and say: "Find the doll wearing the *same* sock."

2. Play this game with the class: Have each student take off one shoe and place it in a pile of shoes. The children form a circle around the pile. The teacher holds up one shoe from the pile and asks: "Who has a shoe that is the *same* as this?"

H. CARTONS AND BEADS

Materials: egg carton and beads of various sizes (2–4 of each size)

1. Give the child an egg carton in which beads have been grouped by size.

2. Give the child another set of beads of various sizes and say: "Place each of these in the right section, that is, in the section that has a bead that is the *same* size."

I. HOPSCOTCH

Materials: chalk; 2 identical sets of at least 8 pictures; index cards; paste

1. On a cement part of the playground draw a chalk hopscotch board. Place a picture in each square.

2. Paste a duplicate set of the pictures on index cards.

3. Tell each child: "Pick a card and hop to the square with the *same* picture."

J. MATCHING HALVES

Materials: Super Snap Cards (James Galt and Co., Cheadle, England) or face pictures you have cut in half

1. Match half-faces or put together Super Snap Cards to show the child.
2. Mix them up and then have the child pick out and put together halves that match.

K. CONCENTRATION

Materials: Concentration Game or playing cards

1. Use a commercial Concentration Game or make your own. You need eight to twelve playing cards (four to six pairs).
2. Place all the cards face down. Tell the children they may each turn up two cards during their turn. If the cards match, or are the same, they can keep them and take another turn. If they do not match, they must be turned back over and the turn goes to the next player.

L. WALLPAPER

Materials: 4–8 patches of wallpaper (some matching, some one of a kind)

1. Place several (four to eight) pieces of wallpaper in front of the child. Some pieces should be one of a kind; others should have matching pieces.
2. Say: "Put together all samples that are the *same*."

M. DOMINO MATCHING

Materials: picture dominos (1 set)

1. Open a set of dominos, preferably one with pictures.
2. Have the children play the game by matching dominos end to end. Tell them: "Put the ends that are the *same* together. Try to make as long a line as you can."

N. LOTTO

Materials: lotto game

1. First, give all children a lotto card and ask them to put the numbered disks (or squares) you give them on the numbers that are the same on their cards.
2. Then, play the game as usual.

O. BODY TALK

1. Ask the children questions to help them understand points of symmetry (pairs) in their bodies. For example: "What color is your left eye? Your right? Both are brown. They are the *same*."
2. Do the same with fingers, toes, socks, etc., and stress, each time, that they are the *same*.

P. COLOR GAME

1. Ask one child to stand.
2. Then ask the class the color of the standing student's socks.
3. Ask all others with the *same* color of socks to stand.
4. Continue this procedure with other articles of clothing. Be sure to ask different children to rise.

Q. OBJECTS THAT ARE THE SAME

Materials: several sets of objects (pencils, paper clips, crayons, cups, balls)

1. Form several sets of common classroom materials: pencils, paper clips, crayons, etc.

2. Hold up one set of objects. Ask the child to hold up the *same* number of the *same* object.

3. Continue through the sets of objects.

R. TEXTURE MATCHING

Materials: soft, hard, and rough objects (2 of each)

1. Gather several *soft* (e.g., cotton balls, sponges), *hard* or *smooth* (wood, glass), and *rough* (sandpaper, bark) items.

2. Ask the child: "Which items feel the *same*?"

3. If playing in a group, let each participant make one match.

S. SOUND SERIES

Materials: tape (cassette) and tape player

1. Using a cassette recorder, make a tape with a series of sounds on it. After each series, leave a pause of about fifteen seconds. Examples of series include: knocking on door, ringing bell; knocking, knocking; etc.

2. Ask the children to clap hands when all the sounds in a particular series are the *same*.

OBJECTIVE 7

MATCHING

Objective: The child will group objects, pictures, sounds, or shapes into sets that have common properties.

Before beginning, explain: Sometimes things belong with each other. For example, pears belong with bananas because they are both food. Children belong with parents. The games we will play help us to understand what belongs with what. When something belongs with something else, we say it *matches.*

A. COLORS

Materials: crayons (3 or more sets)

1. With three to five complete sets of crayons, have the child put all of one color in a pile, all of another color in another pile, etc.
2. Have the child continue until all colors have been separated.

B. SHAPES

Materials: shapes of various colors and sizes

1. Give child a collection of shapes.
2. Ask for sorting by (a) color, (b) shape, and (c) size.

C. PICTURE SORT

Materials: pictures from magazines (several from 3 to 4 categories); index cards; paste

1. Cut pictures from old magazines and paste them onto index

cards. Include pictures of food, clothing, toys, animals, and other categories of interest to children.

2. Ask the child: "Can you sort these pictures so that those in the same category (give example) are together?"

D. DECK SORT

Materials: playing cards (1 deck per child)

1. Give the child a deck of playing cards.

2. Say: "Sort these so that all hearts are together; then all spades; then all clubs; then all diamonds."

3. Next, ask that the cards be sorted by numbers.

E. EGG CARTON

Materials: bag of items (e.g., buttons, marbles, coins, beans, pasta, chips, rubber bands, jacks, etc.) and egg carton

1. Give the child a bag full of items such as buttons, marbles, coins, beans, pasta, chips, rubber bands, etc. Also give the child an egg carton.

2. Say to the child: "Sort these items into the sections of the carton."

F. DICTATING OBJECTS

1. Say a list of objects, such as: boat, car, paper, train, staples.

2. Ask the child which objects go together.

3. Repeat the list using objects from other categories (e.g., school and food).

4. You may bring in objects when feasible.

G. MAGAZINES

Materials: magazines; scissors; paste; index cards

1. Give the child some magazines.

2. Say: "Find pictures of the following things, cut them out, and paste them on cards: pets, toys, animals, houses, cars, etc."

H. SOUNDS

Materials: cassette recordings of animal sounds and of daily routine sounds; cassette player/recorder

1. Record sounds of different animals (cat, dog, cow, lion, etc.) and from the child's daily routine (food being fried, stapling, school bells, table being set, ambulance, playground sounds, etc.).

2. After each sound, ask the child which category it goes in: animal or human.

3. Develop other categories and repeat the steps.

4. You may make picture cards to go with the sounds and have the children classify the cards.

OBJECTIVE 8

RHYMING

Objective: The child will identify words that rhyme when he hears them.

Before beginning, explain: Box and fox sound alike in a way when we say them—they rhyme. Today, we're going to play games that help us understand rhyming. So you must listen carefully as we say words today.

A. POEMS

Materials: rhyming poem

1. Explain that two words that sound alike are said to *rhyme*. Give examples: house, mouse; box, fox; etc.
2. Read a poem that rhymes. After each line or two, ask which words rhymed.

B. RHYMING CARDS

Materials: pictures from magazines of objects with names that rhyme; index cards; scissors; paste

1. Cut pictures from old magazines of objects with names that rhyme, and paste them on index cards.
2. Place mixed cards on table and ask the child to pick two that rhyme. (A variation of this game can be played with the group. Hold up one card and say: "This is a mouse. Can you find a picture of something that rhymes with it?")

C. WORD RHYME

Materials: lists of rhyming words

1. Tell the child: "I am going to read a list of words. Clap your hands once when you hear a word that rhymes with another word in the list."

2. Each list should be of three or four words and only two of the words should rhyme. Read the list through twice.

D. RIDDLES

1. Make up riddles for which children must supply a rhyming word.

2. Examples are:
I rhyme with stool. You can swim in me. What am I? (pool)
I rhyme with make. You like to eat me. What am I? (cake)
I rhyme with see. You like to climb me. What am I? (tree)

E. NAMING RHYMERS

1. Say the word *mouse*.

2. Then say to the child: "Please name all the words you can think of that rhyme with that word."

F. RHYMING BINGO

Materials: bingo boards with at least 6 pictures on them (see example): 1 set of pictures that rhyme with the pictures on the boards (see example); bowl; chips or buttons

1. Distribute bingo boards to children so that each child has a board. Hand out chips or buttons as well.

2. Place the set of rhyming pictures into a bowl and mix them up.

3. Pick a picture from the bowl and hold it up for the class. Ask children to find a rhyming picture on their boards and to place a chip on the square with the picture.

4. The first child to complete his board is the winner.

G. RHYME MATCHING

1. Read each of the following statements to the child and wait for the response.

a. Name an insect that rhymes with *three.* (bee)
b. Name an animal that rhymes with *hat.* (cat, bat)
c. Name a flower that rhymes with *close.* (rose)
d. Name a number that rhymes with *skate.* (eight)
e. Name a letter that rhymes with *tea.* (p, z, e)
f. Name a color that rhymes with *sled.* (red)
g. Name a person that rhymes with *other.* (mother)
h. Name a number that rhymes with *shoe.* (two)
i. Name an animal that rhymes with *dog.* (hog)
j. Name an insect that rhymes with *my.* (fly)
k. Name a piece of clothing that rhymes with *goat.* (coat)
l. Name a letter that rhymes with *tray.* (a)

OBJECTIVE 9

UNDERSTANDS CONCEPT OF OPPOSITE

Objective: The child will be able to demonstrate an understanding of the concept of opposite.

Before beginning, explain: If you are not *little,* you are *big.* These words, *big* and *little,* are opposite. The games we'll play today help us understand what is opposite.

A. MY LAST WORD

1. Explain the concept of opposite and give an example: the opposite of up is down. Tell the child that you are going to read a sentence in which he must fill in the last word, which is an opposite.

2. Sentences that can be used include:
"A pickle is sour, candy is ________."
"A rocket goes up, rain comes ________."
"When you smile you are happy, when you cry you are ________."

B. DAY AND NIGHT I

Materials: opposite cards (Instructo Flannel Board Opposite Card, available from Instructo/McGraw-Hill, Paoli, PA 19301)

1. Make opposite concept cards: cut pictures of opposite things from magazines and paste them on index cards. (You may use commercial opposite cards.) Then separate them into two groups—one for you and one for the child.

2. Hold up your cards one at a time. Ask the child to find its opposite in his group of cards.

C. DAY AND NIGHT II

Materials: opposite cards

1. Use opposite cards from Activity B.

2. Ask the child to pair the opposite cards by himself.

D. FACES

Materials: happy and sad faces (1 of each per child)

1. Give the child a happy and a sad face, each on a separate card.

2. Tell the child that you are going to be saying pairs of words. (Some should be alike—daisy, rose; some opposite—night, day.) When the pairs are opposites, the child must hold up the sad face; when they are alike, the happy face. This activity may also be used with the group.

E. FACES, A VARIATION

Materials: tape of pairs of words; tape player; happy and sad faces (1 of each per child); crayons

1. Prepare a tape on which pairs of words are said. Some should be alike (apple, orange), some opposite (fire, ice).

2. Give the child a happy face and a sad face to color. Say: "Color on the happy face when you hear words that are alike. Color the sad face when you hear words that are opposites."

F. TIT FOR TAT ON THE FLANNEL BOARD

Materials: pictures of opposites for the flannel board (10 or more); flannel board

1. Prepare sets of opposite flannel pictures.
2. You work with one set, give the child the other.
3. When you place a picture on the board, the child must find its opposite and press it next to the picture.
4. Do this with the whole set of flannels.

OBJECTIVE 10

UNDERSTANDS CONCEPT OF SEQUENCE

Objective: The child will put objects or pictures in correct order and be able to tell what he has done.

Before beginning, explain: When we go over what we did at the end of the day with Mom or Dad, we should say what we did first, next, and last. This is the order or sequence these things happened in. The games we'll do today help us put things into the right order.

A. FIRST THIS, THEN THIS

Materials: set of 3 cards that shows sequence (commercial cards called DLM Sequence Cards available from Developmental Learning Materials, P.O. Box 4000, One DLM Park, Allen, TX 75002)

1. Make a set of three cards that shows a sequence. For example: one card could show a foot with a stocking, one could show a bare foot, and one could show a foot with a shoe.
2. Put the cards in order for the class by placing them in sequence on the board. Explain that these cards tell a story and, in any story, the parts of the story are in a certain order.
3. Jumble up the sequence cards and ask one child at a time to put them back in order.

B. JELLO

Materials: items to make jello or a salad and cards that show steps of preparation

1. Make a simple dish, such as jello, in front of the children. As you work, explain what you are doing. (If you do not have

very hot water and a refrigerator, you may want to make a fruit salad instead of the jello.)

2. Next, make sequence cards showing the steps involved: e.g., boiling water, pouring water and jello into a bowl, putting the bowl in the refrigerator.

3. Jumble the cards and ask the children to put them in sequence.

4. Give everyone some of the dish.

C. STORYTIME

Materials: a favorite story; blackboard; chalk

1. Read the children one of their favorite stories.

2. Then ask one child: "What happened first?" If he has trouble, give clues. Draw a picture showing the child's answer on the blackboard.

3. Ask another child: "What happened second?" Draw the answer on the board.

4. Ask another child: "What happened last?" Draw the answer on the board.

5. Repeat the process over several days until all children have had a chance to respond.

D. FIELDTRIP MEMORIES

1. Take a class trip: e.g., to the zoo, on a walk through the woods. Point out memorable events to the children during the trip.

2. Upon returning to the school, ask each child to recount the events that took place. Make sure the account is in correct order.

E. NUMBER CARDS SHUFFLE

Materials: an index card for each of the numbers 1–5

1. The child must know numbers 1 through 5 to play this game.
2. Prepare five index cards, one for each of the numbers in the 1–5 sequence.
3. Give the child the five cards and ask that they be put in order.

F. CIRCLE THREE

Materials: paper (8½″ x 11″) with three circles of different sizes (1 sheet per pupil); paper (8½″ x 11″) for each child; paste; scissors

1. Prepare a one-page ditto that has three circles of different sizes.
2. Ask the child to cut out the circles.
3. Then, take the largest circle and paste it onto a blank sheet of paper.
4. Now, ask the child to paste the other circles in order of size onto the sheet.

G. THE OLD PAPER BAG TRICK

Materials: paper bag and 3 items to put in bag

1. Place three items in a paper bag while the children are watching.
2. Close the bag and ask the group: "What went in first?" "What went in second?" "What went in last?"

H. JUST FOLLOWING DIRECTIONS

1. Give the child a two-part direction: e.g., "Put away the toy on the bottom shelf and then color quietly at your desk."

2. When the child is able to perform the two parts in sequence, give a three-part direction: e.g., "Take off your coat, hang it up, and then take a block game from the shelf."

I. REPEATING

1. Say to the child: "Repeat the words that I am going to say. Say them back to me in the same order."

2. Then say three words: e.g., "cat, bird, mouse."

3. When the child can repeat three in correct sequence, move to four, five, and so on.

J. ADDING ON

1. Play a game in which each child in the group has to remember what has been said in a round-robin activity. Start by saying: "I am going on a trip and taking a suitcase."

2. Next, say: "Now, as we go around the class, each of you must say what I just said plus whatever anyone else has added to it *plus* you must add something you'd take on the trip." Give examples: "You might, for example, take a dog, a cat, pants, sweaters, and so on." They will understand after you go around the group once.

K. BIG TO LITTLE ON THE FLANNEL BOARD

Materials: 3–6 felt cutouts of different sizes and flannel board

1. Have ready several (three to six) felt items of different sizes.
2. Say to the child: "Put these on the board in order of size."

L. THE RESTAURANT

1. This game is for two children. Ask one child to be a waiter or waitress in an imaginary restaurant. Ask another child to be the customer.
2. Tell the customer: "Come in, sit down at the table, and wait for your waiter. When he comes, order whatever you want: for example, you may want soup, crackers, an order of fries, and a hot dog."
3. Tell the waiter: "When you take the order, you must repeat it back to the customer exactly as he gives it to you."

OBJECTIVE 11

FOLLOWS PATH THROUGH MAZE

Objective: The child will follow a simple maze or line to practice eye-hand coordination.

Before beginning, explain: Today, we are going to work on moving through a path without touching the sides of the path.

A. CHALK MAZE

Materials: chalk or blocks

1. On the playground, draw a simple maze with chalk on the concrete.
2. Tell each child: "Walk through this maze but do not step on the lines."
3. You may also build a maze of blocks.

B. MATCHBOX CAR TRACK

Materials: easel paper; felt marker; matchbox cars (1 per player)

1. On easel paper, draw a maze with a magic marker that is large enough for a matchbox car to go through. Put the paper on the floor.
2. Tell the child: "Drive your car through this track until you come back out. When there is an obstacle, you must go *around* not through it."

C. MATCHBOX CAR RACE

Materials: easel paper; felt marker; matchbox cars

1. On easel paper, make a simple path (see example) wide enough for two matchbox cars at the start. Put a dotted line down the middle of the track. As the track comes to an end, make it so narrow that only one car will pass. Place the paper on the floor.
2. Have the child drive the car through the track, staying within the lane chosen at the start. Emphasize: "You cannot touch the solid black lines."

OBJECTIVE 12

RECOGNIZES MISSING ITEMS

Objective: The child will use complete sentences to express himself when asked to tell "what is missing."

Before beginning, explain: When we look at something, we can tell if it is all there. For example, if we look at a dog and it doesn't have one ear, we know right away that something is missing. The games we will play today will help all of us to figure out things that are missing.

A. CHALK FACE

Materials: blackboard and chalk

1. Draw a large face on the blackboard. Put only a mouth on the face.
2. Ask the children: "What is missing?"
3. As they name things, put them on the face.

B. MISSING PARTS

Materials: magazine pictures; scissors; envelope; bulletin board; pins

1. Cut out pictures of animals, people, plants, etc., from magazines. Then cut something off each of these: e.g., a tail, a head, the trunk. Put these parts in an envelope.
2. Pin the pictures on a bulletin board. Ask the child: "Can you name this (animal, object, person, etc.)?" Then say: "Find the missing part in the envelope and pin it up where it belongs in the picture." Help with the pinning, if necessary.

C. WHAT'S MISSING?

Materials: 3–4 sets of 2 identical objects

1. Prepare three or four sets of objects, two objects in each set. Each pair of objects should be identical *except* that one object in the pair has a part missing from it. For example: a handle is missing from a cup, an eraser is missing from a pencil, lines are missing from a piece of paper.
2. As you display each set, say: "Discuss what is missing." Encourage full sentences by questions such as: "How can you tell that is missing? Why do you need a handle on a cup?" etc.

D. TAKING IT OFF

1. Ask one pupil to stand in front of the group. Tell the class: "Look closely at ________ (child's name). Notice what he is wearing."
2. Ask the child to go out of the room with you. Remove an article of the child's clothing (e.g., a sock, shoe, hair ribbon, belt).
3. When you both return to the room, say: "Tell me what ________ (child's name) is missing."

E. GONE

Materials: 3 or more items

1. Place three items on the floor and give everyone time to look at them.
2. Have the children close their eyes while you remove one.
3. Ask one child: "What is missing and how do you know?" Encourage full sentences.
4. Increase the number of items involved as the group progresses.

OBJECTIVE 13

EXPRESSES SELF IN COMPLETE SENTENCES

Objective: The child will express himself in complete sentences when talking about a picture or story.

Before beginning, explain: Today, when you are asked a question, try to answer in more than one word. For example, if I asked, "What color is your hair?" don't answer, "brown." Say, "My hair is brown." That is a sentence. A sentence is something that anyone could understand even if they hadn't heard the question. For example, if you said "brown" to a stranger, he wouldn't know why you said the word, but if you said, "My hair is brown," he would know what you mean.

A. MEMORIES FROM A STORY

Materials: story; drawing paper; crayons for each child

1. Read a simple story.
2. At the story's end, say: "Draw a picture of one thing you remember from the story."
3. Then say: "Tell me about the picture."

B. A PICTURE IS WORTH A THOUSAND . . .

Materials: magazine picture of action taking place; blackboard; chalk

1. Show class an action picture from a magazine or book that they could identify with easily.
2. Ask each child to tell you one thing about the picture and list what is said on the board.

3. Read back this list to the children. Ask the group: "What does our talk today tell you about pictures?" Encourage full sentences in the discussion.

C. NOT A CLUE

Materials: picture cards (1 per youngster)

1. Give each child a card with a picture on it. (Animals, household or school items, and toys all work well.)

2. Say to the children: "Look at your card and turn it face down."

3. Now say: "Everyone will have a turn at describing what is on his card. But, do not actually say the name of what is on the card. We have to guess." Then proceed.

4. If this activity is too hard for some children, you or a classmate can help with clues.

D. THE STORY

1. Tell a story without an end. For example: "There once were two boys, Peter and Paul. They were always together. They went to the movies together. They played together. One day, Peter couldn't be found . . ."

2. Ask: "How do you think this story might end?" Encourage children to answer in full sentences.

E. WHAT PICTURES SUGGEST

Materials: language development cards (*Peabody Language Kit,* Level I, American Guidance Service, Publishers' Building, Circle Pines, MN 55014)

1. Show the class a language development card.

2. Say to the class: "Look closely at this picture."
3. Then ask questions about the picture that will elicit full-sentence responses (e.g., "What is the boy doing?" "What makes you think that's so?").

F. PICK AND TELL

Materials: 6–10 objects

1. Put a variety of toys or objects on a tray or table top.
2. Ask the child to pick one. Then say: "Now describe it." Prompt the child, if necessary, with questions: "What about size? color? use?"

G. BOOKS WITHOUT WORDS

Materials: picture books

1. Find picture books in the library with no text.
2. Give various children the books to look through.
3. Then say: "Tell our class the story in the book." Prompt, if necessary, with questions.

H. ALL ABOUT US

1. Arrange children in a circle and ask them to stand, one at a time, and tell one thing about themselves.
2. Encourage the use of full sentences.

I. TELL A TALE

Materials: felt people; felt objects; flannel board

1. Put felt people and objects on a flannel board.

2. Tell the child: "Make up a story about these people and things on the board and tell it to the class."

J. LONG DISTANCE

Materials: toy telephones (2)

1. Put one child at one toy telephone and another child at another phone.
2. Tell the children: "Carry on a conversation with each other." You may give them a subject: e.g., what they did the day before, favorite game, TV show, pet, etc.
3. If this is too hard, the teacher should be on one phone rather than a classmate.

K. SEEING WITH FINGERS

Materials: shoe box; scissors; items for box

1. Take a shoe box and cut a hole in the lid that is large enough for a child's hand.
2. Place an item in the box, but don't let the child *see* what it is.
3. Then say: "Put your hand in the box and describe what you feel."
4. Ask the child: "What do you think's in the box?"

L. TV

1. Ask children to try to watch a particular television show. You might send a note home to this effect so parents will cooperate.
2. The next day, discuss the show: "What was it called?" "Who was in it?" "What was it about?" "Where did it take place?" "How long was it?" etc.

M. JUST SUPPOSE . . .

1. Ask the class "what if" questions. For example: "What if you came home from school and no one was there?" "What if you found a wallet with lots of money in it?"

2. Encourage the use of complete sentences as children answer.

N. FINISH THE SENTENCE, PLEASE

Materials: easel; paper; felt marker

1. Open a discussion by asking the children, one at a time, to finish a sentence that you start. For example: "My mother gets angry when . . ." or "Love means . . ." or "When I am naughty, my parents . . ." Write the first part of the sentence on the easel.

2. Write all answers on the easel under the first part of the sentence.

3. After all children have answered, read the finished sentences.

O. STORY DRAMA

Materials: story

1. Read a simple story that the children already know, such as "The Three Pigs."

2. Then, choose characters (first pig, second pig . . .) and have the children use words and movement to act out the events critical to the plot.

P. THE WALK

Materials: easel paper, easel, and marker; or blackboard and chalk

1. Take a walk with the class.
2. Then, when you're back in school, say: "Tell me what happened on our walk."
3. Write responses on the board or easel as the children talk. Then read back.

Q. DRAWING STORIES

Materials: easel; paper; felt marker

1. Have one child at a time a draw a picture at the easel.
2. Then say: "Tell me about the picture."
3. Record at the side of the picture what the child tells you and read it back.

R. PUPPET CONVERSATION

Materials: puppets (3–5)

1. You and the child each select one or more puppets.
2. Then suggest to the child that you have a conversation through the puppets.

S. CAN'T HAVE ONE WITHOUT THE OTHER

1. Tell the children: "I am thinking of a garbageman. Now you explain to me all the things that go with a garbageman. For example: A garbage truck goes with a garbageman."
2. Continue with other subjects once the children name all that goes with a garbageman.

T. DESCRIBING

1. Complete a sequenced action such as bending over, touching your toes, and standing up again.

2. Tell the child: "Describe what I did in complete sentences." If the pupil has trouble, give prompts. For example: "What did I do first?" Then do what went first. "What did I do second?" etc.

OBJECTIVE 14

ATTENDS TO SOUNDS

Objective: The child will be able to give attention to sound as evidenced by his ability to identify, classify, repeat, define, or associate what has been heard.

Before beginning, explain: The activities we'll do today will show me what good listeners you are. What do we need to be good listeners? Ears! So, open your ears and here we go. . . .

A. SIMON SAYS

1. Play Simon Says and give only two commands at a time. For example: "Simon says touch your nose and then touch your toes."

2. Do several practice rounds. Then start the game.

3. When a child misses directions, he must sit down until the next round.

B. BOOM, TINKLE, DING

Materials: 3 or more musical instruments

1. Take out a set of instruments. Start with three at first. After the game is familiar you can increase the number.

2. Name the instruments for the children. For example: "This is a tambourine. This is a bell. These are rhythm sticks." Then let them hear the sound each instrument makes and give them a chance to play them.

3. Then say: "Now close your eyes. When you hear me play one of the instruments, say which one you think it is."

C. SOUNDS

Materials: things to make sounds (paper, whistle, balloon, pencil and pencil sharpener, etc.)

1. Say to the class: "Close your eyes. While you keep your eyes closed, I am going to make a sound. Tell me what I am using to make the sound."
2. Then, tear paper, whistle, clap, blow up a balloon and let the air out, sharpen a pencil, etc. After each sound, allow the children to open their eyes and say what they think it came from.

D. SOUND DIRECTION

1. Tell the child to stand in front of you and to close his eyes. Explain that you are going to clap your hands and you want to be told where the clap came from.
2. Then, clap your hands over the child's head. Wait for a response. Then, clap on the left, the right, below, behind, in front of, etc. Do not clap too close to the child's ears. If the child points to (rather than describing) the direction, you should say: "That's right," and move on.

E. VOLUNTEER

Materials: object to hide

1. Ask for a volunteer. Tell him to leave the room.
2. While the child's away, the rest of the class hides something, such as an eraser.
3. When you bring the volunteer back into the room, explain: "We've hidden something. You must find it. To help you, we'll clap our hands—softly when you're away from it, loudly when you're close to it." The child must search until the object is found.

F. HEAR AND DO

Materials: record and record player

1. Tell the class you will play a record and that you will adjust the volume continuously. When it is loud, they must clap their hands. When it is soft, they must put their fingers to their lips.
2. After children catch onto the game, give them each a turn at the record player.

G. SPOON STORY

1. Tell the class: "I'm going to tell you a special story. Every time you hear the word *spoon* in the story, stand up."
2. Use this procedure with other words and stories.

H. WORDS INTO PICTURES

Materials: taped story; tape player; paper (enough for each child); crayons

1. Tape a story.
2. Tell the class you are going to play a taped story. After they listen, they will have to draw a picture about the story. (You may want to play the story twice.)
3. After all pictures are finished, review the story with the class through the pictures. Point out how different people chose to draw different aspects of the story and how they all had used their imaginations in drawing their pictures.

I. SOUNDS LIKE JOHNNY

Materials: tape and tape player/recorder

1. Record the voice of each child saying the same phrase: e.g., "The dog jumps over the log."

2. Play the recording to the class. After each voice, ask the children whose voice they think they heard.

3. This procedure can be employed with street sounds, school sounds, home sounds, etc.

J. BOUNCE COUNT

Materials: simple game boards for each child; buttons or chips (1 per child); ball

1. Give each child a copy of a simple game board and a button or chip to move.

2. Say to the class: "Each time I bounce the ball, move your chip one space on the game board. If I bounce three times in a row, move it three spaces; if I bounce two times, two spaces; and so on."

OBJECTIVE 15

IDENTIFIES LETTERS AND INITIAL SOUNDS

Objective: The child will be able to identify initial letter sounds in words presented and recognize letters when presented.*

Before beginning, explain: Today, we will start to learn some letters you need to know before you can begin to read.

A. THE LETTER *S*

Materials: blackboard; chalk; ditto sheets of a large dotted *S* (1 per child)

1. On the blackboard, print a capital and small letter from the alphabet: Ss. Tell the children the name of the letter and then say: "It looks like a snake. The first letter in the word *snake* is *S*. Also, the month we go back to school after summer vacation starts with this letter. Does anyone know that month? (Pause) Right, *September*."
2. Make an *S* on the board with a dotted line. Have one child at a time come to the board and trace over the dots.
3. Hand out ditto sheets with a dotted *S* that students can fill in at their desks. Make sure all children begin the letter at the appropriate starting point.
4. Say: "You have now learned the letter *S*, which makes a hissing sound when you say it—just like a snake. Can you think of some other words that start with the *S* sound?" Let children give you as many as they can and write these on the board.

*The activities in this section show how to introduce one specific letter. The important information for children to learn in Objective 15 is letter recognition (not reading), since all schools have their own reading programs.

Underline the initial *S* in each entry on the board. (To prompt, give hints such as "I am thinking of a number that starts with *S*.") Be sure to point out any names within the group that start with *S*.

5. Once the children have mastered the letter *S*, you can use this activity to introduce other letters.

B. HOPSCOTCH LETTERS

Materials: chalk and index cards of uppercase and lowercase letters that have been studied

1. Draw hopscotch board on the cement part of the playground. Fill the squares with the upper- and lowercase letters that have been studied (Ss, Tt, etc.). Have duplicates of these pairs printed on index cards.

2. Ask children to form a line in front of the hopscotch board. Then, let one student at a time take a card. Tell the child: "Name the letter you've taken and then hop to all the squares with that letter in them."

3. The children who cannot name the letter must go to the end of the line without hopping. If on the second draw they can't name the letter, give clues. For example: "What letter hisses like a snake?"

C. MUSIC AND LETTERS

Materials: chairs; letter cards; music

1. Set up the classroom for musical chairs, only make sure a chair is available for each child. Place a letter card with a letter they have studied on each chair.

2. Say: "When the music starts, everybody walk around the circle of chairs until it stops. Then, sit immediately. Then, in turn, I'll ask you to hold up your letter card and name the letter."

3. Children who cannot name their letters in three turns should be told their letter and are out of the game.

D. TRAIN FARE

Materials: chairs; letter cards; box

1. Arrange chairs to resemble seats in a train.
2. Put pairs of letter cards (e.g., *S* and *s*) in a box and mix them up.
3. Say to the class: "To board this locomotive, you have to find two letters that match that you may use as a ticket. The letters can be two small letters, two capitals, or a small and a capital letter."

E. HEY, GIVE ME A WORD FOR THAT

Materials: letter cards

1. Hold up a letter the class has studied.
2. Ask: "Timmy, can you name a word that starts with this letter?" Continue with other students and letters.

F. PICTURE CARDS: SOUNDS LIKE . . . ?

Materials: picture cards of objects with names that begin with letters studied

1. Have ready cards with pictures of things whose names begin with letters the children have studied.
2. Ask one child: "What letter does the word for this picture begin with?"
3. Go around the room until you get a correct answer.

G. GLITTERING LETTERS

Materials: black or blue construction paper (1 piece per student); pencils for each student; white glue; glitter or sequins

1. Have each child print a capital and a small letter (e.g., Ss) on a large piece of dark construction paper.
2. Have the children go over the letter with white glue.
3. Now, have them sprinkle the glue with glitter.

H. LETTER MOLDS

Materials: plastic letters and clay

1. Have children press plastic letters they have learned into moist clay and then remove them.
2. Let the molds dry.

I. LISTENING AND FINDING

Materials: letter cards (capitals and small letters)

1. Place letter cards, of both capital and small letters, face up on a table. The cards should be fairly close to one another.
2. Whisper a letter in a child's ear, specifying *capital* or *small,* and say: "Find that letter."
3. If the child picks correctly, he gets to take the letter card off the table and whisper another letter in a classmate's ears. If wrong, the teacher (or whoever preceded the child's turn) whispers the next letter.

J. WAXY WINDOWS

Materials: glass wax and mirror or window

1. Rub glass wax on a mirror or window that the child can reach.
2. Call out a letter and ask a child to reproduce it in the wax.

K. BACK TRACE

1. Ask the child to stand with his back toward you.
2. Trace a letter on the student's back with your finger.
3. Ask the child: "Which letter did I write?"

L. SCAVENGING

Materials: letter cards and shoe box

1. Put several letter cards in a box. Explain the idea of scavenger hunts.
2. Have a child pick one card and name the letter.
3. Then say, "Okay. Now find something in the room with a name that starts with that letter. Go!" (Make sure ahead of time that proper items are out.)

M. SHOWTIME

Materials: chairs; plastic letters; tape; letter cards to match plastic letters (1 per child)

1. Before reading a story out loud, or some other activity that requires the students to listen, arrange chairs to look like a theater.
2. Tape a plastic letter on each seat.
3. Then, give each child a letter card and tell the class: "This is your theater ticket. It has your seat letter on it. Find your seat."

N. ALPHABET SOUP

Materials: plastic letters; soup kettle; large spoon

1. Have children put pairs of matching plastic letters in a soup kettle and stir them up with a spoon. Emphasize the idea of letting the soup simmer.

2. Each child will take a letter from the "soup." Everyone must allow the class to see their letters.

3. Say: "After you draw your letter, look around at the letters other people have. If you see that someone has a letter that matches yours, you can take that letter from them. If your letter is taken, draw again."

O. INVISIBLE LETTERS

Materials: cotton swabs; lemon juice; paper (enough for each child); candle; matches

1. Put cotton swabs and a dish or bottle of lemon juice on a table.

2. Say: "Everyone dip a swab in this lemon juice and use it to write a letter on your piece of paper."

3. When the juice dries, the teacher holds each paper (carefully) over a lighted candle until the letter appears.

4. Ask the class, as each letter appears: "What is the letter?" (Papers can also be taped to a sunny window and the letters will appear.)

P. ROUGH CUT

Materials: sandpaper; scissors; paper; crayons

1. Cut letters out of sandpaper.

2. Let the children feel the shapes.

3. Then, have each child put a piece of paper over a letter, and rub the paper with the side of an unwrapped crayon until the letter appears.

Q. BIG LETTERS

Materials: oaktag; felt marker; scissors; paint; grass or soapflakes

1. Draw an outline of large letters (six-inch) on oaktag. Then have children cut letters out.

2. Let them mix paint with grass or soapflakes and apply the concoction to the letters. Or, have them make collages on the letters with pictures.

R. FEEL IT

Materials: sandpaper letters; bulletin board or blackboard; blindfold

1. Blindfold a child.

2. Put the sandpaper letter on the board.

3. Lead the child to the board and have him feel one of the letters and tell you what it is.

S. MIXED UP

Materials: 3 jars with lids; felt marker and paper to make labels; tape

1. Collect several jars with lids. Make labels with capital letters and corresponding small letters.

2. Label each jar with a capital letter and each lid with the corresponding small letter.

3. Remove lids and mix them up. Ask the children to find the right lid for each jar.

T. LETTER WALK

Materials: large piece of paper (5 feet) and felt marker

1. Draw a huge letter (two to four feet) on a piece of paper.

2. Place the letter on the floor and say to the children: "Walk this line and say, over and over, the letter it forms." Tell the children that these are the size of letters on billboards, signs, and movie screens.

U. FINGER LETTERS

Materials: finger paints; soap and water; paper (1 or more sheets per child)

1. Have ready fingerpaints and soap and water.

2. Assign each child a letter to make by dipping a finger in the paint and then drawing on a piece of paper.

CHAPTER 2

Math Readiness

OBJECTIVES IN CHAPTER 2

Objective	Number of Activities	Page Number
1. Identifies top, bottom, and middle	12	61
2. Identifies above, below, over, under	8	65
3. Classification	18	69
4. Understands before, after, and between	7	76
5. Uses ordinal numbers (first, second, third, etc.)	13	79
6. Distinguishes many, few; more, less, equal	10	84
7. Understands more, less, equal	9	88
8. Counts to 10	8	92
9. Understands, recognizes, and writes numbers	30	96

While a child may be able to tell his parent that he wants *more* ice cream, he may be unable to relate the concept of *more* to other situations. This chapter offers 115 activities to help the pupil learn first to recognize and then to generalize basic quantitative concepts like *more* and *less*.

The activities are designed to help children discover for themselves how a problem that is quantitative may be solved. Consequently, these activities stress concepts rather than information. This chapter's primary goal is to help students begin to discover their abilities to reason as well as to remember.

Classification, matching, and comparison games are included in this chapter as they were in the last chapter. Here, however, the emphasis is clearly quantitative and the material prepares children for beginning numerical activities.

All the objectives in Chapter 2 lead to basic work with whole numbers. The beginning objectives in this chapter generally will be the easiest to teach; the later objectives the hardest.

The same teaching recommendations offered at the beginning of Chapter 1 apply to this chapter. Those children who are unprepared for these activities should be given individual work to bring them to the level required for participation.

Although the activities are designed for either group or individual instruction, the emphasis here is clearly on group work. (There are enough activities to provide the teacher with three per week during the school year.) The teacher should spend as much time as necessary to familiarize the children with new vocabulary as it arises in the activities. For example, explain words such as *sets* and *counters*. Emphasize the game-like quality of these activities and help the children to have fun while they are learning!

OBJECTIVE 1

IDENTIFIES TOP, BOTTOM, AND MIDDLE

Objective: The child will identify the top, the bottom, and the middle of a page.

Before beginning, explain: Today we are going to learn about top, bottom, and middle. Let me see you place your hand on the top of your head. On the bottom of your feet. On the middle of your arm. Good! As we play today, you will see that almost everything has a top, a bottom, and a middle—no matter how big or how small it is.

A. HALF THE BOARD

Materials: 2 wool strips; flannel board; 3 or 4 felt pieces

1. With a strip of wool or string, make a horizontal line to divide the flannel board in half. Explain that there are now two parts of the board—a top part and a bottom part.
2. Give the child several felt pieces and ask that one of them be put on the top half of the board, another on the bottom half, etc. For example, say: "Place this circle on this half of the board, the *top* half. Place that square on the other half, the *bottom* half. Place the triangle on this half."
3. Then, divide the flannel board into thirds. Ask the child to place pieces on the top, bottom, or in the middle.

B. PICTURES

Materials: magazine pictures

1. Locate magazine pictures that have objects recognizable to the child in the top, middle, and bottom of the page. To help,

point out the top, middle, and bottom of the pictures for the child.

2. Ask the pupil: "What do you see at the bottom of the magazine picture?" "In the middle?" "At the top?" Repeat with other pictures.

C. SHAPE AND PASTE

Materials: construction paper; felt marker; scissors; paste

1. Cut out of construction paper enough circles, squares, and triangles for students to have one of each. Shapes should be no longer than two inches.
2. Give each child a piece of paper with horizontal lines that divide it into three sections.
3. Say to the children: "Paste the square on the top of the page; the triangle in the middle; the circle on the bottom."

D. SHELF SPACE GAME

Materials: bookcase with 3 shelves; 3 objects, such as a toy, a book, a ball

1. Locate a bookcase with three shelves.
2. Say to the child: "Here is a toy. Put it on the top shelf. Here is a book. Put it on the bottom shelf. Here is a ball. Put it on the middle shelf."

E. WALL WORK

1. Have the child face the wall.
2. Then, say: "Tell me what is on the top of the room. What is on the bottom?"

F. SIMON SAYS

1. Play this game with the group after basic work on top, bottom, and middle has been done.
2. Say to the children: "Simon says touch the top of your foot. Touch the top of your head. Touch the bottom of your foot. Touch the middle of your hand." Continue with similar directions to the group.

G. TOY TOUCH

Materials: small toy animal

1. Give the child a small toy animal.
2. Then, say: "Touch the top of his head. Touch the bottom of his foot. Touch the middle of his back."

H. ON THE TOP!

1. Locate objects that children can sit on or kneel on safely.
2. Then (for example), say: "Sit on the top of my desk. Sit on the top of the counter, the table, the floor."

I. ABOUT THE SCHOOL

1. Take the children to a common object on the playground or street.
2. Say to them (for example): "Show me the top of the slide, the bottom. Show me the top and bottom of the car, of the door, or the street lamp."

J. TOWERS

Materials: 3 cubes, each a different solid color

1. Use three one-inch cubes, each of a different color. Build a tower with the cubes.
2. Ask the child: "What color's on top? What color's in the middle? What color's on the bottom?"
3. If playing with several children, change the position of the tower's components and give other children a chance to answer.

K. PICTURE THIS, IF YOU WILL

Materials: piece of paper with ball drawn on bottom, house drawn on top

1. Draw a ball on the bottom of a sheet of paper, a house on the top. Display the picture.
2. Ask: "Where is the ball? Where is the house?" The child must give you the words *top* or *bottom*. This is the first activity in which you do not say the words for the student.

L. ANCHORS AWAY

Materials: pan of water; 3 objects that float; 3 objects that sink

1. Set out a pan of water and present the child with several objects that will float (e.g., plastic ball, bar of soap, pencil) and several that will sink (e.g., stick of gum, porcelain cup, penny).
2. Let the child experiment. Then say: "Tell me what went to the bottom. What stayed on top?"

OBJECTIVE 2

IDENTIFIES ABOVE, BELOW, OVER, UNDER

Objective: The child will be able to identify, when asked, the position of an object as being either above or below (over or under).

Before beginning, explain: If I stand here and hold my hand *over* this boy's head (demonstrate) and you see me, you might say: "The teacher's hand is *above* his head." *Above* is the same as *over*. So if I ask you to put your hands *above* your head, I want you to put them *over* your head. Try it.

If you see me stick my hands *under* this desk, you might say: "The teacher's hands are *below* the desk . . . we can't see them." *Below* is the same as *under*. So, if I ask you to put your hand *below* your chair, I want you to place it *under* the chair.

A. STAR BRIGHT

Materials: felt house; felt star; flannel board

1. Place a house (or other object) in the middle of the flannel board.
2. Give the child a star and prompt: "Place the star above the house. Place the star below the house. Is the star under or over the house?"

B. CIRCLE EXCHANGE

Materials: paper and crayons for all

1. Divide the class into thirds: group 1, group 2, group 3. Give out paper and crayons to all.
2. Ask everyone to draw a circle in the middle of the paper.

Then say: "Group 1 and group 2 exchange papers. Now group 3 exchange with group 1. Draw a star above the circle."

3. Exchange again and ask the students to draw a house below the circle.

C. JUST GUESS WHERE THE CRAYON IS

Materials: chair and crayon

1. Explain to the child: "You will sit in a chair, close your eyes, and then someone will hold a crayon either above or below your head. You have to guess which." Then sit the child in a chair and begin.
2. Whisper to another child to put the crayon above the first child's head.
3. Then ask: "Can you guess where the crayon is?" The child must answer either above or below. The use of the words is more important than a correct guess.
4. If the child guesses the position, he gets to be the one who holds the crayon. If not, the child must continue to sit.

D. TABLE'S MIDDLE

Materials: object child can handle (e.g., glass) and table or desk

1. Seat the child at a table (or desk). Give him an object.
2. Say to the child: "Put the object above the table. Now, put it below the table."

E. LEAP OR CRAWL

Materials: jump rope

1. Ask two children to hold an end of a jump rope so that it is about one foot off the floor.
2. Tell the children, one at a time, either: "Jump over the rope." Or: "Crawl under the rope."
3. Then ask each child if he was above the rope or below the rope.

F. BRIDGE'S MIDDLE

Materials: blackboard and chalk

1. On the blackboard, draw a bridge. Then draw a boat below and a plane above the bridge.
2. Ask the group, "Where is the boat? Where is the plane?" They must answer either "below" or "above" the bridge.

G. BOX AND CRAYON

Materials: crayon and shoe box

1. Hold a crayon above a box.
2. Ask the child: "Is the box above or below the crayon?"
3. Then say: "Is the crayon above or below the box?" Change the crayon's position and repeat questions. Then continue with other objects.

H. ROPE GAME

Materials: rope (width of classroom)

1. String a rope from one side of the classroom to the other at about the height of the children's heads.
2. Then say: "Those with noses above the rope sit down. Now, those with noses below the rope sit down." Change the height of the rope and continue with feet, arms, shoulders, etc.

OBJECTIVE 3

CLASSIFICATION

Objective: The child will classify objects by kind, color, shape, size, or use, when asked.

Before beginning, explain: If you see a lot of things on the table in a restaurant, you would be able to see that some of them belong together. For example, french fries and beans would belong together because they're both vegetables. Chicken and hamburger would belong together because they're both meats. Salt and sugar would belong together because they're both spices. Today, we are going to see how to decide what things belong together.

A. SORT THE COLORS

Materials: 3 shoe boxes with a different color of circle on each and 15 index cards with colored pictures from magazines (colors correspond to circles)

1. Set out three shoe boxes, each with a circle of a different color pasted to the front.
2. Also, paste pictures from magazines on index cards. Have pictures of one color each that match the colors of the circles.
3. Place the cards in a pile. Say to the child: "Sort these into the boxes so that the color of the circle matches the color of the picture."

B. SHAPE SORT

Materials: 3 boxes, with a circle pasted on the front of one, a square on the front of another, a triangle on the front of the third; magazine pictures with those shapes; index cards; paste

1. Set out three boxes with a circle pasted on the front of one, a square on the front of another, and a triangle on the front of the remaining box.
2. Cut out pictures that have these shapes and paste them on the index cards (e.g., pictures of a ball, a grapefruit, an orange, a clock; pictures of a television, a box of cereal or raisins; pictures of a triangle, a wedge of cheese, a slice of pie).
3. Place the cards in a pile. Say to the child: "Sort these into the boxes so that the shape of the picture matches the shape pasted on the front of the box."

C. DOMINO GROUPS

Materials: set of picture dominos

1. Have ready a set of picture dominos.
2. Say: "Place the pictures that are the same next to each other. Try to make as long a line of dominos as you can."

D. ROW BOAT

Materials: 6 red felt boats; 6 blue felt boats; flannel board

1. Put two rows of three boats (or other shapes) on the flannel board. Each row should be a different color.
2. Have a number of boats that match the two colors on the board. Hand one of the boats to the child and say: "Place it in the proper row."
3. Continue with the other boats.

E. MULTISORT

Materials: 30 pegs of different colors and a mix of 20 blocks and beads of different shapes and colors

1. Have available a pile of pegs of different colors. Ask the child to sort by color.

2. Have available a mix of beads and blocks and ask the child to sort them by color or shape or both.

F. TWINS

Materials: 6 picture cards, each with 2 pictures or shapes—some have the same picture twice, some have two different pictures

1. Make six or more picture cards. On each card, have two pictures or shapes. On some cards, the pictures should be the same. On the other cards, the pictures should be different.

2. Say to the child: "Organize these cards into two piles: one pile for all cards on which the two pictures are the same; one pile for cards on which the two pictures are not the same." Demonstrate, if necessary.

G. WHAT DO WE SHARE?

Materials: 10 or more squares (or other shapes) that differ in color, texture, design, etc.

1. Gather and display a variety of one kind of object (e.g., squares). The objects should be about the same size, but different in color, texture, design, and so on.

2. Hold up two of the objects that vary in color. Ask: "What do these two share?" Or, "How are these the same?"

H. SHAPE HUNT!

Materials: 10 pairs of shapes, cut out of construction paper or cardboard

1. Hide one of each of the ten shapes about the room.
2. Explain to the children: "We are going to hunt for shapes around the room. When I raise a shape in the air, I'll call out several of your names. Those children whose names I've called out must move quietly about the room, find the cutout that matches mine, and bring it to me."
3. Begin the game. After each group goes, ask the children to tell how the objects are alike.

I. HAT TRICK!

Materials: blackboard and colored chalk

1. Draw several hats of differing colors on the blackboard.
2. Say to the class: "If any of you are wearing something that's the same color as the hat I point to, please stand up."

J. UP DOWN

Materials: blackboard and colored chalk

1. Use colored chalk to draw nine objects on the board (plane, fish, whale, bird, ball, etc.). Also draw a bridge on the board.
2. Tell the children: "When I touch one of these pictures, you tell me whether it is thought of as being above or below the bridge."

K. GO TOGETHER

Materials: enough picture cards for the class, each with a different picture on it (some of the pictures should be in the same category—e.g., kitchen things, office supplies, toys, animals)

1. Pass out a variety of picture cards or objects to the class.

2. Tell the group that you will ask class members to come to the front of the room—one by one—and hold up their cards. If anyone else feels that his card goes with the one being displayed, he should hold it up.

3. When children hold up their cards, ask: "Why do you think your card goes with this one?"

L. THINK!

1. Say to one child: "Tell me all the things we ride in."

2. After the answer, ask the class for other things to ride in that were not listed.

3. Proceed with things that give light, things to wear, things to eat, garden tools, etc.

M. NO WAY!

Materials: doll dishes (cups, plates)

1. Use a set of doll dishes. Place two cups and a plate in a row.

2. Ask the child to point to the one that does not belong and say: "No way!"

3. Ask the child: "Why does it not belong?"

4. Continue with other rows.

N. FILL-IN

1. Tell the children that you will say a group of words and then, when you pause, they must say a word. Give an example: "If I say, 'a pair of ________,' you could say 'shoes, scissors, or pants,' to finish what I began."

2. Continue:
a class of ________ (children, boys, girls, etc.)
a bunch of ________ (carrots, celery, bananas, etc.)
a bottle of ________ (milk, juice, etc.)
a jar of ________ (baby food, honey, etc.)
a box of ________ (cereal, candy, etc.)
a can of ________ (peas, beans, soup, etc.)
a bag of ________ (peanuts, candy, etc.)
a pound of ________ (coffee, sugar, etc.)
a pail of ________ (water, sand, etc.)
a bowl of ________ (soup, cereal, etc.)
a team of ________ (players, horses, etc.)
a group of ________ (boys, girls, etc.)
a pile of ________ (books, papers, etc.)

O. WHAT'S THAT?

1. Tell the children that you are going to name something and that they must tell you what kind of thing it is. Say to them: "For example, I say, 'Football is a kind of ________.' You say, 'Game.' "

2. Continue:
cow is a kind of ________ (animal)
dress is a kind of ________ (clothing)
dime is a kind of ________ (money)
red is a kind of ________ (color)
uncle is a kind of ________ (relative)
hammer is a kind of ________ (tool)
orange is a kind of ________ (color or food)

P. YOU TELL ME!

1. Tell the youngsters you are going to say three words and they must say, immediately after, the group the words belong in. Say to the class: "For example, I will say, 'dog, cat, monkey' and you say 'animal.' "

2. Continue:
orange, peach, pear (fruit, food)
store, school, house (building)
river, ocean, lake (water)
bracelet, necklace, ring (jewelry)
pencil, pen, chalk (writing instrument)
car, airplane, train (transportation)
shoe, sweater, dress (clothing)
happy, sad, mad (feelings or emotions)
dentist, doctor, veterinarian (medicine, healing)
teacher, principal, custodian (people at school)

Q. GET OUT!

1. Tell the children you are going to read a list and they must tell you which word should get out of the list because it doesn't belong. Say, for example: "If I say 'dog, cat, monkey, tack,' you would say 'tack.' "

2. Continue:
lunch, supper, breakfast, *cat*
meat, potatoes, *fly,* salad
nickel, penny, *mother,* quarter
father, brother, *dog,* sister
bandage, *chair,* thermometer, medicine
car, chair, table, bed

R. BUILDERS

1. Tell the children you are going to say a word and they must tell you if it refers to an object made of wood or glass.

2. These are the words: *bookcase, vase,* seesaw, *cup,* windshield, baseball bat, mirror, *desk,* lightbulb. (NB: the words italicized may be wood or glass objects. Child should be given credit for either use.)

OBJECTIVE 4

UNDERSTANDS BEFORE, AFTER, BETWEEN

Objective: The child will demonstrate an understanding of before, after, and between.

Before beginning, explain: When we talk to our friends about the day we had, we may start with what we did when we first got to school in the morning—*before* lunch. Then, we talk about what we did *between* lunchtime and the end of class. And then we talk about what happened *after* school. *Before, between,* and *after* are very important ways to describe how we spend our time.

But these words are also important in describing how we place ourselves in line at school—they describe *where*. Some of us stand *between* others. Some of us come *after* everyone else in line. Some of us come *before* anyone else in the line.

We'll practice using these three words as we play today, to describe *where* and *when*.

A. VERTICAL SANDWICHES

1. Ask a boy to stand. Then ask a girl to stand in front of him and another girl to stand behind him.
2. Ask another pupil: "Who is before the boy? Who is after?"
3. Continue with other children.
4. Expand the concept to objects.

B. HIDE WITH NO SEEK!

1. Ask children to stand before (in front of) and behind objects in the room.
2. Use doors, desks, chairs, etc.

C. LIFE

1. Remind children that before and after are also used with time. Then ask questions that involve activities with which the child has been or will be involved.

2. For example: "What did you do before school; after school yesterday; before lunch? What will you do after June; before you sleep?"

D. PICTURE POSITION

Materials: 3 simple pictures, blackboard or bulletin board; tape

1. Tape three pictures on the board in a row: e.g., a boy, a bird, a dog.

2. Point to the pictures from left to right and tell the child what is first, second, and third.

3. Ask the child: "What is before the second picture? What is after the second picture? What is between the first and third pictures?" Continue with questions of this sort.

E. OLD NOAH

Materials: 6 or more small toy animals (in proportion to each other if possible)

1. Tell children the story of the Ark. Then line up a row of toy animals: e.g., a dog, a cat, an elephant, a mouse.

2. Ask the child: "What animal's before the dog? (None!) After the cat? At the end? In the middle?"

F. ALL CHILDREN

1. Line up all youngsters in the class.

2. Ask questions such as: "Who's before the girl in the red sweater? After the boy with the blue jeans? Who has no one after him?"

G. JAZZ AND JAM SESSION

Materials: 3–5 musical instruments

1. Take out the instruments. Give one to each of three to five youngsters.

2. Ask them each to play, one at a time.

3. Then ask: "What instrument was played before the bells? Before the recorder? Before the drums? After the bells?" etc.

OBJECTIVE 5

USES ORDINAL NUMBERS

Objective: The child will put events in order of occurrence using ordinal numbers (first, second, third, etc.).*

Before beginning, explain: Today we will learn some other words for our numbers: one, two, three, and so on. When you are number one in a line, you may say, "I'm number one," but you also may say, "I'm first!" When you are two, you may say, "I am second." When you are three, you may say, "I am third." Can you tell me what 4, 5, and 6 would be? How about 7, 8, 9, and 10?

A. THE SWITCH

Materials: 3 pictures related to events in a story

1. Tell a story using a series of three pictures. For example: Picture of a boy—"Tom was a boy who could not go out of his room because he had been naughty."
   Picture of window—"But he tried to sneak out of his window anyway."
   Picture of dad—"But his dad caught him and told him he could not watch TV for a week because he tried to sneak out."

2. Mix up the pictures and tell the youngster: "Put the pictures back in order so the beginning card is on the left, over here, and the ending card on the right, over here. As you do this, retell the events of the story using the words *first, second, third.*"

*Most children know how to count by rote when they enter kindergarten from watching children's television programs. Therefore, it is safe to introduce ordinal numbers at this point. If, however, you find a child who has not mastered counting, do not teach this skill until counting is perfected.

B. SOUND OFF

1. Line up three children.
2. Ask the class: "Who is first? Second? Third?"
3. Increase the number of children in the line.
4. Then say: "When I ask 'Who is first?' the first person in the line says, 'I am first.' We will continue in the same way with second and so on." Play.

C. CHOO-CHOO

Materials: enough chairs for each child

1. Tell children that you are going to line up their chairs so they are arranged like cars on a train.
2. Ask each youngster to sit down. Explain that you are going to ask various children to step out of their cars, which means they should get out of their seats.
3. Say: "First car—step out."
4. Continue with "second car, third car," etc.

D. TOUCHING

1. Tell children: "Watch carefully as I touch my body." Then touch three or four parts of your body.
2. Then ask: "What was touched second? First? Third?" Repeat as necessary if children have difficulty remembering.

E. THE OLD PAPER BAG TRICK

Materials: paper bag and 3 items to put in the bag (toy, ball, paper clip)

1. Say to the children: "Watch carefully." Then place three items in a paper bag, one at a time.

2. Ask: "What did I put in first? Second? Third?"

F. SIMON SAYS

1. Play the game. Tell youngsters to touch their noses first, knees second, etc.

2. Then ask: "What did you touch last? First? Third? Second? Fourth? Repeat the activity using different parts of the body.

G. MY STEPS

1. Line up children by size.

2. Explain that they are in line in order of size. Tell them: "When you hear a clap, run freely around the room until I say *stop*."

3. Clap your hands. When you say *stop*, make sure original order is gone. Then tell children to go as quickly as possible to a line where they are in order of size.

4. Go down the line and ask each child to tell you his position (first, seond, etc.).

H. FIRST THIS! SECOND THIS! THIRD THIS!

1. Tell the child to perform a series of three actions: e.g., raise hand, jump up, then sit.

2. Then ask the child: "What did you do first? And second? And third? Now tell me what you did from start to finish."

I. ONLY THE HAIRDRESSER KNOWS . . .

Materials: 3 or more small dolls of different hair and/or skin color

1. Line up several dolls that differ in appearance.
2. Say to the youngster: "Name the position of each doll. For example, 'the blond-haired doll is first.' "

J. SNACK TIME

Materials: food for snacks

1. At snack time, tell children to watch as the basket of cookies (or treats) is passed.
2. Then ask: "Who got the second cookie?" Continue.

K. ROWS

Materials: blackboard and chalk

1. Draw these three rows on the blackboard.

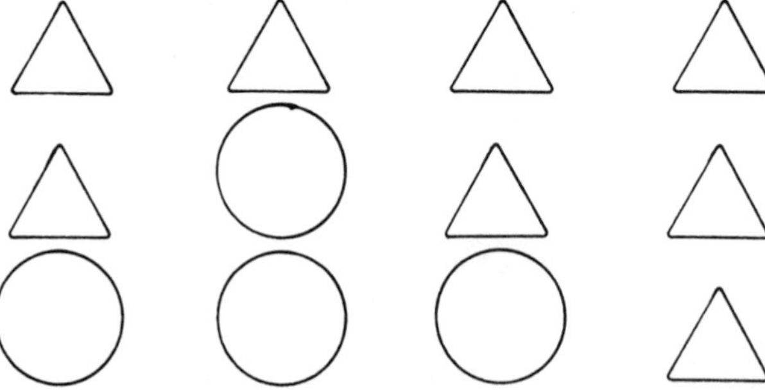

2. Ask the child: "How are these rows different? Which shape is different?" Encourage the child to respond with an ordinal number.

L. LITTLE HOUSE ON THE BLACKBOARD

Materials: blackboard and colored chalk

1. Draw three houses on the blackboard using different colors.
2. Ask the child: "What color is the first house? The second house?" etc.

M. DRAWING THINGS

Materials: paper and crayons for each child.

1. Ask the children to draw various things in specific order.
2. For example, say: "First draw a red square, second draw a yellow cross, third draw a blue circle."

OBJECTIVE 6

DISTINGUISHES MANY, FEW; MORE, LESS; EQUAL

Objective: The child will distinguish between many and few, more and less, and most and least. The child will identify equal.

Before beginning, explain: When you say, "I have *many* toys," you mean you have a lot of toys. But if you said, "I have *few* toys," you'd mean that you don't have a lot. If you say, "I have the same number of toys as my friend," you mean that you and your friend have an *equal* number of toys.

But if your friend has 5 marbles and you have 2, your friend has the *most* marbles and you have the *least*. He has *more* marbles than you have. You have *less* than he has.

Many/few, most/least, more/less, and *equal* are important words to describe how many or how much of something we have without using numbers.

A. PENCILS AND BUTTONS

Materials: large number of buttons (10 or more) and small number of pencils (4 or less)

1. Show the child a group of buttons and pencils. The pencils should be far fewer in number than the buttons.

2. Help the child decide which pile has many objects and which has few. Then say: "Show me which pile has *more* objects, and which pile has *less*."

B. GIVE MORE . . .

Materials: 25 bottle caps and 2 boxes

1. Give the child some bottle caps and two boxes.
2. Say: "Put *many* caps in one box and a *few* in the other."

C. WATER PITCHER

Materials: 2 identical glass pitchers or glasses and water

1. Have ready two identical glass pitchers. Before the child, pour water into one until it is one-third full; pour until the other is two-thirds full.
2. Ask: "Which has *more;* which *less*?"

D. WINK OF AN EYE

Materials: 4 buttons or chips

1. Place four buttons or chips on the table. Have the children look at them.
2. Then say: "Close your eyes." When their eyes are closed, take one button away.
3. Say: "Okay, open your eyes. Are there more or fewer buttons now?"
4. Increase in difficulty by using more buttons.

E. STAND UP I

1. Ask one girl and two boys to stand.
2. Count them out loud: "One, two, three."
3. Then ask the class: "How many boys do you see? How many girls?"
4. Then: "There are more boys than girls. How do we know?"

F. STAND UP II

1. Ask two boys and two girls to stand.
2. Explain to the class: "The number of boys and the number of girls is equal—it's the *same*."
3. Next, increase the number of members in each group and ask questions about size.
4. Finally, have the class in two equal groups. Ask the class: "Which group has more? Which has less?" Prompt them to say "equal" if necessary.

G. CLOTHING EXAMINATION

1. Say to the children: "Look at each other's clothing."
2. Ask: "Which color are most of us wearing?"
3. Then move on to other questions using the same concepts. For example: "Are most of us wearing long or short sleeves? Who has the most pockets? Who has as many pockets as Tom?"

H. PLEASE RETRIEVE

Materials: classroom objects, such as books

1. Say: "I have five books here on my desk. ________ (child's name), now get less (or more) than five." Continue using other objects.

I. ROWS

Materials: flannel board and felt cutouts (10)

1. Put an unequal number of items in two rows on the flannel board.

2. Ask the children: "Which row has fewer items?" "Which has more?"
3. Then ask: "Can anyone make the rows equal?"
4. Let them show you.

J. CHILD CHART

Materials: easel; paper; felt marker

1. On the easel, write down the child's responses to these questions:
   The color I like most is ________.
   The color I like least is ________.
   The most exciting thing that has happened to me is ________.
   The TV show I like the least is ________.
2. Do this for each child and keep the responses.

OBJECTIVE 7

UNDERSTANDS MORE, LESS, EQUAL

Objective: The child will match two sets of objects and explain that one set, in relation to the other set, has more or less or an equal number of objects.

Before beginning, explain: Let's count the number of children here. OK. If we have exactly that many cups for snack time, then we have an *equal* number of children and cups. If we put down one more cup than there are children, we have *more* cups than children. If we take one cup away, we have less cups than children. Equal, more and less are important ideas to know.

A. FLOWER VASES

Materials: flannel board; 3 felt flowers; 3 felt vases

1. Place three felt vases on the flannel board and then put a felt flower in each vase.
2. Point to each vase and tell the pupils that the flowers match the vases and each vase matches a flower.
3. Then say: "There are as many flowers as vases. There are as many vases as flowers. These sets are equal."
4. Take one flower away. Explain: "There are now more vases than flowers. There are less flowers than vases. The sets of vases and flowers are not equal."
5. Continue with other items: e.g., apples and trees or dolls and dresses. Have the children explain matching and equal to you.

B. FIVE ROWS

1. Call five children to the front of the room and have them

stand in a row shoulder to shoulder.

2. Ask another five children to come up and find a person to stand behind.
3. Ask them: "Are there as many children in the back as the front? Are the two groups equal?"
4. This game can also be played with one row of boys and one of girls, if desired. As a variation, call up either four or six children for the back rows. Ask questions about more and less.

C. STRAW VOTE

Materials: 5 straws and 5 cups

1. Have five straws together and five cups together.
2. Ask the children to raise their hands if they think there are as many straws as cups.
3. Ask one child to place a straw in each cup.
4. Now point out that there are as many cups as straws, and as many straws as cups. There is an equal number of each item.
5. Next, ask four children to come up. Ask the class: "Are there as many cups and straws as children?" Have each child pick up a cup with a straw to demonstrate. Explain that there are more cups and straws than children.
6. This game may also be played with cups and saucers.

D. MATCHING

Materials: 4 cubes of the same color and numerous other loose objects from around the classroom

1. Hold up four one-inch colored cubes.

2. Say to the child: "Find an equal number of objects of another kind." You may make the game harder by requiring a color match and a number match.

E. FOLLOW DIRECTIONS, PLEASE

Materials: cubes (5 per child) and patterns for cube placement (1 per child)

1. Give each child five cubes.
2. Draw patterns on separate sheets of paper for arranging three cubes. Have a different pattern for each class member, if possible.
3. Say: "Arrange your cubes according to the pattern. Be sure your cubes match the pattern."
4. Continue activity with four and five cubes.

F. CRACKER BOWL

Materials: 2 bowls and crackers (1 per child)

1. Display a bowl with crackers, enough for each child to have one.
2. Ask: "Do you think there are enough crackers for everyone in the class?"
3. Then say: "Let's find out." Have each child say his name out loud. As it is said, remove a cracker from the first bowl and put it in the other bowl.
4. Continue this activity until all crackers are in the other container. Then ask: "Is there a cracker for each child?" Let the children eat the crackers.

G. EXACT!

Materials: routine items, such as scissors, cups, pencils (1 per child)

1. Have individual children gather enough scissors for the group, enough cups for a group snack, enough pencils for a group activity.
2. Ask, after each collection of items: "Is the number of items (scissors, cups, etc.) equal to the number of children in the room?"

H. STRINGS

Materials: flannel board; 5 felt birdhouses; 5 felt birds; 5 strings

1. Place five birdhouses (or other cutouts) on one side of the flannel board and five birds (or other cutouts) on the other side of the board.
2. Ask children if there are as many birdhouses as birds.
3. Then, place one string between each birdhouse and bird to show that the items are equal.
4. Now: "Do the number of birds equal the number of houses?"

I. FIVE MEN MATCH

Materials: flannel board; 5 felt men; many felt cutouts, including at least 5 hats

1. Place five men on the flannel board.
2. Ask one child at a time to find as many hats as there are men from a collection of cutouts. As each hat is found it should be placed on top of a man's head.

OBJECTIVE 8

COUNTS TO 10

Objective: The child will understand the concept of counting and will count from number 1 through number 10.*

Before beginning, explain: When we want to know how many children are here, we have to *count*. Count with me. (When you finish counting, explain the following.) The last number we said tells us how many are in our group. There are _______ in our group of children.

A. COUNT OBJECTS

Materials: flannel board; 5 felt cutouts; cubes or counting chips (5 per child)

1. Place a set of five objects on the flannel board.
2. Provide each child with five cubes or counting chips. Remind the children that when we count a set, or group, of objects, the last number we say tells how many members are in the set.
3. Say to them: "Watch while I count the items on the flannel board."
4. Then: "Now you count the items on your desks. How many are in your set?"

B. CHIPS

Materials: picture number cards for 1–5 and chips (10 per child)

*We use counting to 5 in this unit, though you should expand the activities to include numbers to 10. It may be necessary, in some cases, to begin by counting only to the number 2.

1. Make a set of picture number cards for numbers 1 through 5 (one picture on the card for number 1; two pictures on the card for number two; and so on). Give each child 10 chips.
2. Then show the children one of the cards for thirty seconds.
3. Turn the card face down and say: "Make a set with your chips that is like the one you just saw."
4. After they can do this activity, ask them to count their chips and tell you how many they have. Remind them of the numbers (1, 2, 3, 4, 5), if necessary.

C. MY OBJECT, BUT YOUR COUNT

Materials: variety of common objects (buttons, cubes, clips, etc.)

1. Place a group of objects on the table (e.g., buttons, cubes, or paper clips).
2. Say to the child: "Pick out three buttons to place in front of you and count them out loud." Then proceed with other numbers and objects.

D. SECRETS I

Materials: egg cartons (1 per child) and small objects to fit in the egg carton divisions (1–5 per child)

1. Give each child a closed egg carton containing one to five objects, only one object in each division.
2. Explain: "We are going to play a secret game. No one will know your secret until you show it."
3. Call on one child to open his egg carton and to tell how many objects are inside.
4. Then say to the child: "Count them as you hold them up."

5. Repeat this procedure with every class member.
6. Exchange cartons.

E. SECRETS II

Materials: same as in Activity D, SECRETS I

1. Put different numbers of objects in each egg carton and distribute closed cartons to the class.
2. Have children open their cartons.
3. Then ask: "Who has the carton with three objects?"
4. Continue, depending on ability of the group.

F. BOUNCE COUNT

Materials: ball to bounce

1. Tell the children to count as you bounce a ball.
2. Then bounce a large ball a varying number of times.
3. After each series, ask: "How many bounces did you hear?"

G. GIANT STEPS

1. Ask one child to stand in front of the room.
2. Explain that you will tell each class member to take a number of steps toward the child. The speed with which they reach the child in front depends on the size and number of the steps they are asked to take.
3. Then say, for example: "Johnny, take three giant steps."
4. The child who reaches the mark first gets to stand at the front of the room in the mark's place.

H. BOARD COUNTING

Materials: blackboard and chalk

1. Draw several objects on the board (e.g., three squares).

2. Ask the child: "How many are there?" This game may also be played with the whole class.

OBJECTIVE 9

UNDERSTANDS, RECOGNIZES, AND WRITES NUMBERS

Objective: The child will understand, recognize, and write the numbers 1 through 10.

Before beginning, explain: Numbers tell us *how many.* If you see one flower, you would think the number 1. The number 1 looks like this. (Demonstrate on the board.) If you saw two flowers, you'd think the number 2. The number 2 looks like this. (Continue with the example of flowers and write the numbers up to 10 on the board.) Today, we're going to begin practicing the numbers from 1 to 10.

A. TRACES

Materials: dittos of numbers (1 per child); dittos of dot numbers (1 per child); pencils or crayons (1 per child); paper

1. Hand out the dittos to the children and explain: "On this paper is the number 1. Trace it with your finger."
2. Then: "On your second piece of paper there are dots. If you begin at the top with your pencil and connect each dot until you reach the bottom of the page, you will see the number 1."
3. Then: "Write the number 1 on your blank sheet of paper."
4. Show children the method of each of these steps on the blackboard, if they run into difficulty. Continue the process with numbers 2 through 5.

B. BLOCK COUNT

Materials: blocks (5 per child) and number cards for numbers 2–5

1. Give each child two blocks.
2. Then, hold up the numeral 2 and explain that this number tells how many blocks they have on their desks.
3. Continue this activity with numbers through 5.
4. Make sure children understand block and numeral relationships before going past number 2.

C. FELT BOARD JUNGLE

Materials: flannel board; 5 felt palm trees; number cards for numbers 1–5

1. Place one to five palm trees on the flannel board.
2. Distribute the five number cards to five children—one card for each child.
3. Tell the group to decide who has the correct number—the one that shows the number of trees. That child should place the numeral on the board.

D. HOLD UP!

Materials: number cards for numbers 1–5 and loose objects around the room for children to collect

1. Explain: "When I hold up a number, I will say someone's name. That person must first tell the number and then find that number of objects (e.g., books) in the room and bring them to me."
2. Play the game. Make sure there are available objects to collect.

E. TWOS

1. Tell the class: "Think of things that normally come in twos, or in a pair. When you are called on, say one of those pairs."

2. Give an example, such as "a pair of socks," and then play the game by calling the first child's name.

F. THREES

1. Tell the youngsters: "Think of the names of stories or songs that have the number *3* in them. When you are called on, say one of those titles."
2. Give an example, such as "Three Billy Goats Gruff," and then play the game.

G. TIME FOR ART

Materials: drawing paper (1 sheet per child), each with the number *1, 2,* or *3* on it and crayons for each child

1. Provide drawing paper for each pupil. On each sheet, print a number (1, 2, or 3) before passing the paper.
2. Tell the youngsters: "Draw as many objects (specify circles, squares, diamonds, etc.) as the number on your paper says to draw."

H. FINGERS

Materials: blackboard and chalk

1. Tell the class that you are going to write a number on the blackboard. When they see what it is, they should hold up that many fingers.
2. Write a number on the board.

I. BLACKBOARD PLAY

Materials: large number cards for numbers 1–5; blackboard; chalk

1. Have large number cards in your hand.
2. Explain: "When I say a name and hold up a number, that person must come to the board and draw as many items as the number on the card. I will say which item to draw (e.g., squares)." Demonstrate if necessary.

J. PICTURE PASTE PIZAZZ

Materials: magazines; paste; scissors; construction paper; pencil or crayon

1. Tell the children: "I want you to look through these magazines. To start, I want you to find four pictures of people, cut them out, and paste them on a sheet of paper on which you have marked a 4. The pictures with the most pizazz get on the board."
2. Continue with other numerals.

K. HOW MANY, PLEASE?

Materials: flannel board; assorted cutouts; felt numbers

1. Place one felt cutout (e.g., a tree or a square) on the flannel board.
2. Ask a child: "How many are there?"
3. Then ask another child to find the correct felt numeral and to place it on the board.

L. NONE

Materials: flannel board

1. Have the flannel board cleaned of cutouts.
2. Point to the board and ask: "How many objects are on the board? None, that's right. The number for none is 0."

*M. PICNIC

Materials: 11 paper plates; felt marker; chips (10 per child)

1. Have a set of paper plates equal to the numerals you are working with (0–10). Place a number on each plate. Begin with 0.
2. Tell the child: "Place as many chips on each plate as the number says."

N. DIRTY LAUNDRY

Materials: 2 chairs; clothesline; 22 clothespins; paper; scissors; marking pen; dot cards with dots from 0 to 10

1. Tell the children you are going to hang out some pretend clothes. Then string a clothesline between two chairs.
2. Have the children cut out paper socks. Then help them mark the socks with numbers between 0 and 10. Put socks on the line.
3. Have ready cards with dots. There should be one card with the correct number of dots to equal each of the numerals on the socks.
4. Tell the class: "Hang the dot card next to its matching sock. The number on the sock should be the same as the number of dots on the card."

O. SQUARE DESIGN

Materials: flannel board; 10 felt squares; felt numbers 0–10

1. Arrange squares on the flannel board as shown (see example).

*Up to this point we have only been working with numbers up to 5. Before continuing, be sure the children are familiar with numbers up to 10. If necessary, go back over activities in this unit and expand them to be used with numbers 6–10.

2. Place the numbers 0 through 10 in random order at the bottom of the flannel board.

3. Point to each group of squares and say: "Find the correct number and place it near the group of squares."

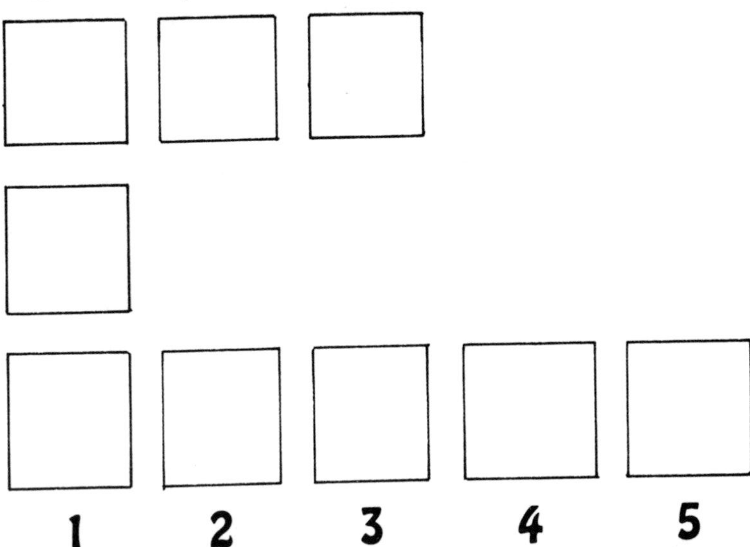

P. THE OTHER SIDE

Materials: number cards for numbers between 0 and 10 (1 card per child) and crayons

1. Give everyone a number card.

2. Say to the pupils: "Draw as many squares on the back of your card as are necessary to equal the number on the front."

Q. CHAINS

Materials: strips of colored construction paper and glue

1. Set out strips of colored construction paper and glue.

2. Ask the pupils to make one-color chains with links equal to the number you are now studying: e.g., 3 red links, 3 blue links, etc. Demonstrate if necessary.

3. Save the chains to add onto with new numbers, or link all the chains together and use for board or room decorations.

R. BREAK IT DOWN

Materials: beans or buttons for counters (25 for each child)

1. Give two or three children a set of twenty-five counters (e.g., beans or buttons).

2. Say to the children: "Arrange these counters into sets of five." Use other numbers as the activity proceeds.

S. FISH

Materials: cards that show from 1 to 5 objects; cards for numbers 1–5; paper clips; string with magnet

1. Make cards that show one of five objects and cards that show numerals 1 through 5. Attach paper clips to the cards.

2. Tell the children: "We are going to play Fish. Your fishing line will be this string with a magnet at the end. When it's your turn, toss the line into the pile of cards and pull out one card. If you can name the numeral or the number of objects on the card, you get to keep the card." Vary the range of numbers as skills grow and children tire of the game.

T. HOPS

Materials: cards with numbers (1 number per card, 1 card per pupil)

1. Give each student a card with a number on it.

2. Then, line up the children in a row. Tell them: "When you come to the front of the line, you have to hop the number of times on your card. If correct, you go sit down. If wrong, you go to the end of the line." Proceed.

U. STICKS WITHOUT ICE CREAM

Materials: popsicle sticks (10 for each child)

1. Give pupils ten popsicle sticks.
2. Then, say: "Make a design on the table using four sticks." Continue with other numbers for designs.

V. DESIGN COUNTS

Materials: counters (same number for each child)

1. Give each child in the class the same number of counters and name the number you gave them.
2. Say: "Arrange your counters any way you like. When you're finished, we'll look at everybody's designs."

W. DOTS!

Materials: number cards for numbers 1–10 and corresponding dot cards

1. Place a set of number cards and a corresponding set of dot cards in various sequences.
2. Say to the children: "Put the number cards in the same order as the dot cards." Then rearrange the number cards into a new sequence and say: "Put the dot cards in the same order as the number cards."

X. BOOKMAKERS

Materials: paper (5 sheets per child) and stapler

1. Have children staple five sheets of paper together along the side.
2. Put a numeral at the top of each page. Then say: "Draw the number of circles that equals the number at the top of each page."
3. The activity may be continued by having pupils cut pictures from magazines and then asking them to paste in the "book" the number of pictures that corresponds to the numeral at the top of each page.
4. Repeat as children know more numbers.

Y. FRUIT CUPS

Materials: numbered cups (1 per child) and raisins (1 box per child)

1. Provide cups with numbers on the front. Have a small box of raisins for each child.
2. Say to the pupils: "Put the number of raisins in the cup that equals the number on the front."

Z. PEGBOARD

Materials: pegboard and 15 pegs

1. Give the child a pegboard and fifteen pegs.
2. Then give instructions, such as: "Put one peg in the top row. Put three pegs in the next row."
3. When there are some pegs in each row, ask the child to go back and tell you what he has done.

AA. PITCH OR HOP

Materials: paper (5 large sheets) and bean bag

1. Put a number on each of five large sheets of paper and place the numbered sheets on the floor.
2. Give the child a bean bag and say: "Throw it to number 5." Continue with other directions.
3. The child also can be allowed to hop to the correct number.

BB. TRAIN CONDUCTOR

Materials: index cards with numbers (one number per card, one card per child); paper punch; chairs

1. Have ready a small paper punch and index cards, each with a number on it.
2. Set the chairs in the room in a row and tell the children to take a seat. Give each pupil a card. Make one child "conductor."
3. Say to them: "You are now on a train. Your card tells how many stops the train will make before your destination."
4. Continue: "Give your card to the conductor when you're asked for it, and he will punch the number of holes indicated by the number." Proceed.

CC. MIND READING

Materials: number cards (1 per child)

1. Give each pupil a number card.
2. Explain to class: "I will say that I am thinking of a number and it's between two other numbers, such as 2 and 4. The child who has the number I'm thinking of must hold up that card. In this case the answer is 3."

DD. CLOTHESPINS

Materials: paper plates (1 per child) and clothespins (5–10 per child)

1. Have ready enough paper plates for each pupil to have one; on each plate write a number between 0 and 10.

2. Tell the children: "Put the number of clothespins around the plate that equals the number on the plate."

CHAPTER 3

Social Studies Readiness

UNITS IN CHAPTER 3

Human beings, according to present theorists, begin their lives as highly self-centered creatures with little awareness of other people's needs or of social structure. By the time they are five or six years old, they have begun to recognize their part in the fabric of humanity. They have become socially conscious. But at this age, the consciousness is still very undeveloped.

This chapter is designed to foster an awareness of each person's part in society. The chapter is divided into units. Unit I helps children begin to see what they have in common with each other. Units II through VIII are designed to help children understand how and why society operates in its present manner. Unit IX is intended to give children a sense of society's dynamic nature—its evolution technologically. Unit X, which is to be used when appropriate during the school year, introduces children to the history behind a number of important holidays.

Each unit is divided into three sections. *Important Ideas,* the first section, may be read to the class by the teacher. It explains the topic that the class will work on in that unit. It is followed by *Discussion Questions* to help the group think about the topic. The 112 *Activities* in this chapter, which occur in the third section of each unit, are ways to help the group explore the ideas.

Approximately one month should be devoted to each of the first nine units. When introducing units, the teacher should take care to clarify terms and introduce vocabulary.

This chapter is important in helping children learn to see themselves as part of a class or group, with responsibilities to that group. Basic training in classroom behavior, therefore, should begin here.

UNIT I

ALL ABOUT ME

Important Ideas: I am me, I'm special, and there is no one just like me. I have a special name that was given to me when I was born. No one has fingerprints or a voice just like mine. I am different from others in some ways and the same in other ways. I can do many things now that I couldn't do when I was very little. I have different feelings at different times; sometimes I am glad, sad, angry, tired. I do not have to be good at everything I do and it is okay for me to make mistakes. Each year I have a special day; it is called my birthday. I have a body that has many parts—eyes, ears, nose, etc. I live with my family.

Discussion Questions

1. How are you different from others in your class?
2. How are you the same as others in your class?
3. What are some of the things you like?
4. What are some of the things you do not like?
5. How have you changed since you were a baby?
6. Even when children look alike do you think they are different from each other when you get to know them?

A. BABY

Materials: baby pictures of youngsters in class

1. Ask children to bring in their baby pictures.
2. Mix up all the pictures. Have one child stand. Then say to the class: "Which picture do you think belongs to this person?"

B. I'M CHANGING

Materials: baby pictures of youngsters in class; drawing paper for each pupil; crayons; bulletin board

1. Discuss physical changes the children have gone through since their baby pictures. Then tell each child to draw a picture of himself.
2. Hang baby pictures next to drawings on the bulletin board.

C. VOICE PLAY

Materials: tape; tape player/recorder

1. Tape record each child's voice (see Chapter 1, Objective 14, Activity I).
2. Play back the tape and pause after each child's voice. Say to the class: "Who do you think this voice belongs to?"

D. MIRROR MIRROR

Materials: mirror

1. Use a hand mirror or, better still, a wall mirror.
2. Tell the children: "Let's look at ourselves in the mirror." Then tell each child: "As you look, describe what you see."

E. HANDPRINTS

Materials: clay or fingerpaints and paper

1. Set out clay or fingerpaints and paper. Ask each child to make a handprint.
2. Have children examine prints and discuss similarities and differences.

F. YOU GUESS

1. Start by explaining: "We're going to play a guessing game. First, I will describe someone in the room. Then, we'll go around the class and each person gets to guess whom I described until someone guesses correctly. The person who gets it right then describes someone else and the rest of us try to guess."

2. Begin with obvious things like sex and dress and hair color.

G. MY GREAT SHAPE!

Materials: roll paper; felt marker; scissors; crayons

1. Ask each child to lie down on paper so that you can outline him.

2. Then have children cut out their own outlines. Encourage children to help each other cut, decorate, and color their outlines.

H. A NAME

Materials: easel; paper; felt marker

1. Make a graph on a large piece of paper with everyone's full

	MIDDLE NAME	GIRL'S NAME	BOY'S NAME	LIKES NAME	FAMILY NAME
Thomas Pat Johnson					
Celeste Alvarez					
Lincoln Thompson					

name. Draw five (or more if you wish) columns after the names.

2. Then ask, and check the appropriate columns: "How many people have a middle name? How many have girls' names? Boys' names? How many like their names? How many are named after a family member?"

I. PEOPLE WHO NEED

Materials: magazines; scissors, paste; string; oaktag

1. Have children make a mobile representing the needs of people. Explain: "People need many different things, like food and love and fun. You think of other things. Go through these magazines and cut out pictures that show the things people need."

2. Have the children paste the pictures on oaktag. Then you connect the pictures with string to make a mobile.

3. Hang up the mobile and discuss it.

4. Ask the children what they each contributed to the mobile, what else could have been on the mobile, and so on.

J. A PANTOMIME

1. Say to the class: "Each person likes to do certain things, like play games, watch TV, go to the movies. I want each person, when I say his name, to get up and act out what he likes to do. Don't use words. We'll guess."

2. Help children think of things if they seem to be having difficulty with the task.

UNIT II

THE FAMILY

Important Ideas: Some families are big and some are small. People who live in families share work and play and help to take care of each other. Parents help children grow up.

Not all families are alike. They do not necessarily consist of father, mother, and children. Some families also have grandparents living with them. Mothers and fathers work hard to give their families food and shelter. People all around the world live in families. In every family someone takes care of small children. Families have problems, too. It is not always easy to live together happily.

Discussion Questions

1. Who is in your family?
2. What do people in a family do together?
3. What special holidays do you celebrate with your family? How?
4. Why must families have food, clothing, and shelter?
5. How do people in a family help each other?
6. Do you think animals live in families?
7. Who is in your family that loves you?
8. Why do we need to have families?
9. Do you do any special jobs at home?
10. Can very small children take care of themselves? Why or why not?
11. What would happen if people in a family didn't help each other?

A. ROLES IN FAMILIES

1. Divide children into two groups. In each group assign the roles of mother, father, children, and grandparents.

2. Have one group silently act out a scene in which everyone is involved in the preparation of dinner. Help the children break the activity into five distinct steps: cooking, setting the table, eating, cleaning the table, and washing dishes.

3. In the other group, everyone should be sitting around watching television except the mother, who is preparing dinner alone.

4. Discuss the two situations. Ask the class: "Does it take longer when one person does all the work? Which family had the most fun? Do you think it is fairer when only mom cooks, or when everyone helps out with dinner? How about other activities like caring for the yard or washing clothes? Should dad help mom with laundry, should mom help dad with yard work?"

B. OUR FAMILY

1. Explain that the class is a family in a way, that we all work and play together for nine months.

2. Then say: "So we must each be responsible for something that benefits the whole class." Assign each child a special job in class: cleaning, plant care, toy custodian, snack helper, blackboard eraser, etc.

C. PORTRAIT: FAMILY

Materials: paper and crayons for each child

1. Tell the children: "In our minds, we each have a picture of the way our family looks. Of people, and pets, and houses or apartments. Draw the picture."

2. Have children discuss their drawings of their families.

D. FAMILY CHART

Materials: paper and crayons for each child

1. Make a chart to show how families fit together and display it for the class. (See sample.)

2. Say to the class: "Now each of you make a chart of your own family. Name your chart. For example, I'll call mine 'The Thomas Family.' " Help children write names on their charts.

3. Compare the charts.

4. Ask children: "Do all families look alike?"

The Thomas Family

mother	father	brother
sister	grandma	dog

E. SOME FIGHT!

Materials: easel; paper; felt marker

1. Say to the class: "Families sometimes have disagreements about work, or dress, or other things. Can you name some of the things members of families fight about among themselves?"

2. Record children's ideas on easel paper and then read them back and discuss in class.

F. TAKE A LETTER

Materials: easel; paper; felt marker

1. Say to the children: "I want each of you to tell me a story about a favorite family activity. I'll take notes."

2. Record stories on the easel and then discuss various points within each story: e.g., How do family members feel about each other when they do this activity? Who does it help most?

G. MAGAZINE HUNT

Materials: magazines and scissors for each child

1. Tell the class: "Look through these magazines and cut out pictures of families—even families of animals (dogs, cats, etc.)."

2. Then discuss the pictures: "How do you think the family gets along? Can you pick out the father, the mother, the children? What are they doing in the picture? Why are they a family? Where do you think they live?" etc.

UNIT III

SHELTER FOR THE FAMILY

Important Ideas: All families need shelter or protection from the elements. A house provides protection from danger and from different kinds of weather. The family home is a place where the members of the family can be together. People live in different kinds of houses. There are private houses, apartment houses, trailers, igloos, log cabins, etc.

Families move to a place where there is work to be done. Some families move to a place where the weather is warm. Families move for many reasons.

Discussion Questions

1. Did your family build its own house? Why not?
2. What do the people living together in your house do for fun?
3. How do your parents help take care of you?
4. What work do you do for your family?
5. What can you do to make your house a happier place?
6. What is used to build houses?
7. What is the difference between a small house and an apartment house?

A. MILK HOUSES

Materials: empty milk cartons for each child; construction paper; paste; scissors; felt markers

1. Give an empty milk carton to each child. Tell the children that they are all going to make houses out of the cartons and cover them with the color of construction paper that is closest to the color of their own house. They can draw in doors and windows with a felt marker.

2. Help the children with their houses. When everyone is finished, put the houses together to form a village of houses. Add churches, schools, fire stations, etc.

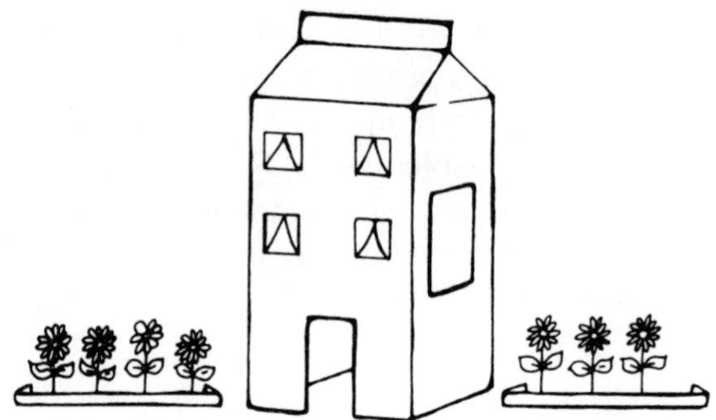

B. MY HOME

Materials: paper and crayons

1. Tell children to draw pictures of their homes.
2. Then, have each child draw a picture of the place inside the home where the family dines; have them show the family at the table.

C. EACH ROOM

Materials: dollhouse

1. Use a dollhouse as a model. Point to a room in the dollhouse and say to one child: "Tell me what goes on in this room."
2. Continue with other children and rooms.

D. OUR EXPERIENCES

1. Ask children: "What different kinds of houses have you lived in?"

2. Select one type of house (apartment house, trailer, etc.) named by each child and say to the child: "Tell me one thing about what it was like to live in that house." (Encourage discussion of motels, camping shelters, etc.)

E. OUR HOUSE

Materials: boxes, blocks, and other materials to construct a toy house

1. Collect boxes, blocks, and other materials to make a toy house.

2. Work together with children on making the house.

3. While you're building the toy house, discuss with children their ideas about homes—what rooms they prefer, what size they feel different rooms should be, what types of houses they like, etc.

F. TOWN WALK

1. Take a walk with the children through the community near the school.

2. As you stroll, point out the different kinds of houses in which people live.

UNIT IV

FOOD FOR THE FAMILY

Important Ideas: All people need food and water to live. Many communities have big stores, such as supermarkets, where people buy food. People can get almost any kind of food they want in these stores.

The stores sell the food for money. But some people grow their own food. Farmers, for instance, grow a lot of their own food, but they still have to buy some food at the store.

Discussion Questions

1. What is your favorite food?
2. What food could you get from a farm?
3. What food do you buy in a store?
4. How do farmers help you get food?
5. Is there another place you get food from? (e.g., restaurants).
6. Could you go for very long without food? What would happen?
7. Why do we need water? What would happen to plants without water?

A. TO BUILD A STORE

Materials: empty food containers and tables

1. Ask children to bring empty food containers from home—jars, boxes, cans.
2. Set up the tables in the classroom to resemble supermarket lanes. Put items on each side of the lanes.
3. Let several children be shoppers and others be cashiers, butchers, stockers, etc.
4. Play supermarket!

B. FOOD COLLAGE

Materials: poster board; felt marker; magazines; scissors; paste

1. Ask children to name their favorite foods. List them on poster board.
2. Then give children magazines in which to find pictures of those food items to cut out.
3. Paste the food item next to its name.

C. MY FOOD

Materials: magazines; scissors; paste; paper plates (1 per child)

1. Tell each child to find a picture of his favorite food in the magazines and to cut it out.
2. Give each child one paper plate and have the child paste the picture on the plate.

D. A DRINK

Materials: magazines; poster board; scissors; paste

1. Have children look through magazines for pictures that show how we use water.
2. Let them cut out the pictures and paste them into a collage on a piece of poster board.

E. MARKET RESEARCH

1. Ask pupils to think of questions they would like to have answers to from people who work in a supermarket. For example: How many kinds of food do they sell? How does meat

come to them? How do they decide how much something costs? What do they sell most? Why don't they sell certain items?

2. Then arrange a trip to the market. Contact the market's manager and explain the nature of the visit.

F. MARKET PEOPLE

Materials: blackboard and chalk

1. Ask children to name the different kinds of workers in the supermarket. List these on the blackboard.
2. Point to each name and ask: "What is this person's job?"

G. MARKET TO FARM

1. Try to arrange to go to a farm.
2. Once there, prompt questions about animals, crops, jobs, taking product to market, seasons, equipment, and so on.

UNIT V

CLOTHING FOR THE FAMILY

Important Ideas: Families everywhere need clothing. People choose clothing that will make them feel comfortable or look nice. The weather helps us decide what clothes to wear.

Long ago, there were no clothing stores and most of the clothing was made at home. Now, most families buy their clothing at stores near where they live. Some people, though, do not go to the store; they use a catalogue and order their clothes by looking at pictures.

Discussion Questions

1. What do you wear when it is hot?
2. What do you wear when it is cold?
3. What are some things you would wear in the rain?
4. What clothes do you wear when you want to be comfortable?
5. What do we get from sheep that we make cloth from?

A. ILLUSTRATING CAPTIONS

Materials: easel; paper; felt marker

1. Tell the children you are going to draw pictures for each of the following captions, but you need their suggestions. Draw what they tell you.
   "Clothes We Wear Indoors"
   "Clothes We Wear in Hot Weather"
   "Clothes We Wear in Cold Weather"
   "Clothes We Wear on Rainy Days"
   "Clothes We Wear at the Beach"

B. RAINY DAY

Materials: paper and crayons for each child

1. Tell children: "Draw a picture of yourself in the outfit you wear on a rainy day."
2. Discuss umbrellas and hats. Are they clothes? Why?

C. PICTURES

Materials: magazines and catalogues with pictures of clothes; scissors; paste; construction paper

1. Pass out magazines and catalogues to all children in the class and have them cut out pictures of different types of clothing.
2. Then tell children to paste their pictures down on construction paper to make a collage.
3. Once they are finished pasting, ask children to hold up their collages, one at a time, and explain why and where people wear the clothes that are pictured. Help them out, as necessary.

D. CLOTHING AROUND THE WORLD

Materials: large picture book showing clothing worn in other parts of the world

1. Show children pictures of clothing worn in other parts of the world.
2. Encourage discussion about the different types of clothing. What is the same or different about the clothes students are wearing and the clothes they see in the pictures? Why might the clothes in the pictures be different? Explain, if necessary, about differences in weather, climate, and customs.
3. For a variation of this activity, bring in pictures of clothing from the past. Encourage the same kind of discussion.

E. ONE ITEM!

1. Tell the class: "When I call your name, say one item of clothing and then tell me when and where it is worn."
2. Prompt individuals as necessary in this activity.

F. CLOTH

Materials: cloth pieces and scraps

1. Collect scraps of many different kinds of fabric.
2. Pass around each piece of fabric and ask the class: "What piece of clothing could be made from this?"

UNIT VI

THE COMMUNITY

Important Ideas: All over the world, people live in communities. In some communities people live close together, and in others they live far apart. In some ways, all communities are alike; in other ways, each community is different from any other. Families live in communities because they want to be near other people. Our neighborhood is the community where we live; it is made up of our own home and nearby buildings.

Discussion Questions

1. Do you think it is important to have friends? Why?
2. What are some ways that communities are the same?
3. What are some ways that communities are different?
4. What happens to communities in a big snowstorm?
5. In what kinds of communities do people live far away from each other?
6. Has anyone been to a farm community? What was it like?
7. How do communities change?
8. Do you like having friends to play with?

A. CLASSROOM MAP

Materials: blackboard and chalk

1. Make a map of the classroom, starting with an outline of walls, doors, and windows.
2. Explain how maps work and point out north, south, east, and west, both in the classroom and on the map.

3. Have children suggest other things that should go on the map —desk, chairs, rugs, tables, coatrack, sandbox, sink, etc.

B. SCHOOL MAP

Materials: blackboard and chalk

1. Take a walk around the school corridors and outdoor play areas. Discuss indoor rooms and what they are used for, and the main features of the schoolyard.

2. Back in class, draw outlines of the school and yard, then have children suggest main features for you to add to the map.

C. SCHOOL NEIGHBORHOOD

Materials: blackboard; colored chalk; drawing paper; crayons

1. Take a walk of several blocks around the school, discussing the names of streets, and key buildings in the neighborhood. Have children point out shops, homes, apartment buildings, churches, etc.

2. Back in class, some children may want to start their own maps. Encourage them to do so by handing out paper and crayons. At the same time, start to outline the streets of the school's community on the blackboard.

3. Have the children suggest the buildings that should be put on the big map. Use different colored chalk for different kinds of buildings—homes, shops, apartments, etc.

4. Go over the names of the streets and their direction and distance from the school. Play a game, asking: "What's the street in front of the school? How many blocks to the church building? the drug store? the body shop?"

5. This can be an evolving activity, involving the children in ob-

serving, mapping, and discussion for several weeks. Encourage children to work on their own maps throughout this period.

D. SHOPPING

Materials: blackboard and chalk

1. Make a list on the board of the stores in the community.
2. Point to a name on the list, read it out loud, and then ask the children: "What does that store sell? Can you tell me in which direction it is located? Have you been there?" Continue with the other stores listed.

E. EXTEND THE FAMILY

1. Ask pupils: "Do you have aunts, uncles, or grandparents who live in another town?"
2. Ask each youngster to describe the town the relatives live in. Ask about size, stores, churches, zoos, movies, ballparks, local customs, etc. Compare that town to the community the school is in.

F. COMMUNITIES IN OTHER COUNTRIES

Materials: large picture book showing towns or cities in other countries

1. Show students pictures of towns or cities in other parts of the world.
2. Examine each picture slowly with the class. Point out similarities and differences in the communities: types of buildings, clothes people wear, methods of transportation, etc.

3. Encourage discussion of these other communities. Would students like to live there? Why or why not? Which community do they like best? Why?

G. IDEAL COMMUNITY

Materials: blackboard and chalk

1. Tell children that you are all going to think up plans together for a new community. Ask them what they would like to have in their community and list responses on the blackboard.

2. You can help guide discussion by first asking for suggestions about size and number of people in the community. Then prompt, if necessary, with questions about buildings, homes, transportation, etc. Be sure each child gets a chance to contribute ideas.

H. MY FRIENDS

Materials: easel; paper; felt marker

1. Go around the class and ask each student to complete the following: "A friend is someone who ________."

2. Write their responses on the easel paper. After everyone answers, read back what's been recorded. Ask if anyone can add more or if anyone does not agree with the things that have been listed.

UNIT VII

FAMILIES AT WORK IN THE COMMUNITY

Important Ideas: The community needs many workers to do various kinds of jobs. It takes many different people in the neighborhood to help us get the things we need. Some workers in our community are people who help us keep well, people who build things for us, people who keep us safe. Some jobs are done by both men and women while others are usually done by only one group.

Some family members need to work to earn money to buy things the family needs, such as food, clothes, and housing.

Some people wear special clothes or uniforms when they work.

Most people are paid for the work they do. Some are given money; others are given checks that they can cash for money. People can put checks or money in the bank to keep it safe until they need it.

Discussion Questions

1. Who wears special uniforms in their work?
2. Who are some of the people in our community who help keep us well?
3. Who are some of the people who build things?
4. Who are the people who keep us safe?
5. Can you think of jobs that can be done by both men and women? (Examples: doctor, newspaper boy/girl, police, salesperson, etc.)
6. Can you think of other people who help in the community? (Examples: construction people, factory workers, newspaper and TV people.)
7. Why do you think some people like their jobs?

8. Can you be a mother and still work at a job in the community?
9. What would happen if no one did any work?
10. What kind of job would you like to do when you grow up?
11. Do you think it would take a long time to learn the job you would like to do?
12. Do you think it is good for your mother or father to work?
13. Where do people learn how to do their jobs?

A. OCCUPATION HATS

Materials: blackboard; chalk; construction paper; scissors; paste; crayons or markers

1. Ask children to name different occupations and list them on the board.
2. Then, assign each child an occupation (that involves a hat) from the list. Help children make hats out of construction paper. (Examples: nurse, fireman, policeman, restaurant employee, bus driver, taxi driver, queen, king, miner, clown, etc.)

B. MY FOLKS

Materials: blackboard and chalk

1. Ask each child: "Who works in your family and what do they do?"
2. Record responses on the board and, after everyone has answered, reread them and discuss.

C. ME, WORK?

1. Ask the pupils: "Does anyone here have a job?"
2. If they answer "no," help each pupil think of some small job to do at home for a week (on a daily basis).
3. Write a note to parents explaining the activity. Ask them to return a note in a week to let you know if the job was done.
4. Give out small rewards when jobs were done.

D. PICTURE THINGS

Materials: pictures of occupations and corresponding items involved in each of the occupations pictured

1. Display all kinds of items that go with jobs: stethoscope, police badge, fireman's hat, hammer, etc.
2. Have pictures of some aspect of the occupations represented by these articles: e.g., surgical ward, squad car, burning building, house under construction, etc.
3. Say to the class: "Match the pictures to the articles on the table."

E. WORKERS TALK

1. Arrange for fathers and mothers with various jobs to come to school and explain their work. Also, invite people from other occupations to visit.
2. Prepare students with some questions to ask.

F. THE SCHOOL BEAT!

Materials: blackboard and chalk

1. Ask students to name workers in the school.

2. List these on the board. Ask children to describe what each worker does.

G. WORKER ROLL

Materials: roll of paper; magazines; scissors; paste

1. Have pupils name fifteen kinds of jobs.
2. Then, on a roll of paper, have them paste pictures from color magazines that illustrate workers at these jobs.

H. PORTRAIT: PARENTS

Materials: drawing paper and crayons

1. Give drawing paper and crayons to children.
2. Say to them: "Now draw a picture of your dad or mom (or other guardian) at work."

I. STORY BOARD

Materials: magazine pictures of people at various jobs

1. Hold up a picture of men and women working.
2. Then say: "Tell me a story about this kind of worker."
3. Continue with other pictures.

J. JOB CONNECTIONS

1. Say to the children: "Different places have different jobs associated with them. When I name a place, you name a job."
2. Name: hospital, police station, fire house, restaurant, ranch, beach.

UNIT VIII

RULES IN THE COMMUNITY

Important Ideas: All groups have rules. This is because people who live together need rules to keep them safe. Rules are sometimes called laws. People need rules so one person doesn't do bad things to others. Rules, in short, help people. This is why people should obey the rules in their community.

Rules are also important to solve fights between people. In our classroom and at home we also have rules. Our nation, the United States of America, has rules just like families do. We choose the people who make rules (laws) for us by voting. The chief leader of our country is the President of the United States. He must follow the rules, as does everyone else elected by the people of the country.

Discussion Questions

1. We learn some rules in school. Where else do we learn rules?
2. What would happen if no one obeyed rules?
3. Have you ever tried playing a game without rules? What happened?
4. What are some rules we have in school?
5. What are some rules you have at home?
6. Have you ever seen a sign that showed a rule?
7. Why is it important to know the rules?
8. What rules would you make for your child?
9. Would you make your child follow the same rules your parents make you follow?
10. Are the rules for children the same as for adults? Which ones? Why? Why not?

A. CLASSROOM

Materials: blackboard and chalk

1. Ask the class: "What would be good rules for the classroom?"

2. Write them on the board and discuss.

B. TRAFFIC

Materials: poster of traffic rules (stop sign, school open, etc.); construction paper; felt markers; scissors

1. Display a poster with traffic signs.

2. Ask the youngsters to identify the signs and the rules they represent. Help them out with the more difficult signs.

3. Then have the children make several traffic signs of their own from construction paper: STOP, BUS STOP, RAILROAD CROSSING, CROSSWALK, etc.

4. Then tell some youngsters to pretend they are riding in a car. They must follow the directions the signs give when they see these signs flashed by their classmates.

C. RECESS

1. Say to the class: "Imagine you are going out for recess."

2. "Now tell me the rules that must be followed on the way out and on the playground."

3. "Why do we have these rules?"

D. OTHER RULES

Materials: blackboard and chalk

1. Say to the pupils: "Think of some rules for a park."
2. List these on the board and then discuss them.
3. Continue with rules for swimming pools and kitchens.
4. Ask. "How are safety rules any different from regular rules in the pool or kitchen?" Ask for examples of the different kinds of rules.

E. GAMES

Materials: simple board games

1. Go around the class and ask each child to tell what his favorite game is (both indoor and outdoor).
2. Let each child explain the rules to the game.
3. Show the children several board games and discuss the rules for each.
4. If there is time, go outside and play some of the outdoor games. Be sure to draw attention to the rules as the children play.

UNIT IX

LONG AGO AND FAR AWAY: THE WORLD IN THE PAST AND IN THE FUTURE

Important Ideas: We learn about the past from pictures, photographs, books, TV programs, and people who lived in the past. In the past, people had different kinds of machines than we do now. There were no cars, so people walked or used horses. People used spinning wheels to make thread, the telephone looked different, and bicycles also looked very different. Long ago most people lived on farms and in small towns. When the little towns began to grow, some of them became cities. Cities are always changing. Many Americans now live in or near a city.

People have always learned to live in new places. They now can live on the North Pole or in a hot desert. They can even live for a while in space, or under the sea.

People have gone to the moon for a few days. The men who have explored the moon are called astronauts. Astronauts are people who travel into space. People have always wondered what it would be like on the moon. However, many things had to be invented before anyone could travel to it. Since there are no water, plants, or animals on the moon, all of these things had to be carried from here. There are no people living on the moon. The astronauts worked very hard to explore the moon. Everyone was very proud of the first men to step on the moon.

Discussion Questions

1. Have you ever seen an old photograph? How did you know it was old?
2. Do you know what the clothes were like in olden days?
3. Why do you think there are no people living on the moon?
4. Why couldn't men in the olden days travel to the moon?

5. What do astronauts wear when they are in space?
6. What could happen to the astronauts on the moon?
7. Why do you think men went to the moon?
8. Would you like to live on the moon?
9. Did you ever watch men going to the moon on TV?
10. Would you like to be an astronaut? Why? Why not?

A. EARLY AMERICA

Materials: large picture book of American settlers and colonial days

1. Show children drawings from a book of colonial days. Point out different ways of dressing and discuss.
2. Show early communities. Ask what is the same in communities now, what is different?

B. WAYS TO TRAVEL

Materials: large picture book of transportation in the early part of the century; paper; crayons for each child

1. Show pictures of ways people used to travel—horse and carriage, early cars, bicycles, trains, etc.
2. Ask children about newer ways to travel. Talk about newer cars, airplanes, rockets.
3. Have each child draw one way to travel—car, boat, plane, walking, etc. Then ask each child to show the drawing to the rest of the class and say if it is old or new or has always been used. Encourage discussion—ask who has travelled that way, is it fast or slow, etc.

C. MOONSCAPES

Materials: paper and crayons for each child

1. Ask the children: "Have you seen TV pictures of what it looks like on the moon? What do you think it really looks like?"

2. Have them draw pictures of what they think the moon would look like if they were standing on its surface.

D. ROCKET MAN

Materials: paper towel rolls (1 per child); construction paper; scissors; scotch tape; aluminum foil

1. Make cones by cutting circles made of construction paper halfway across and then folding them over and taping. (See art below.)

2. Have pupils set cones on top of paper towel tubes and tape into place.

3. Cover entire object (cone and tube) with foil. You now have a rocket for space travel!

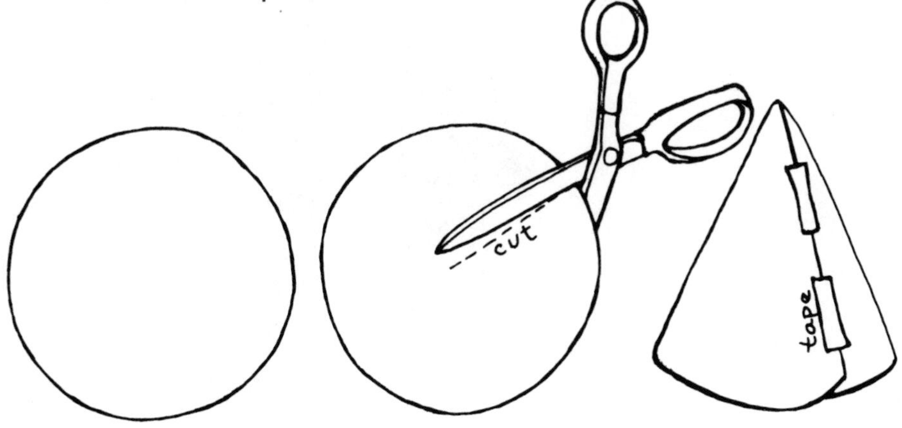

E. MAN FROM . . .

1. Tell the children: "Make believe you have met someone from outer space. What do you think he would look like?"

2. Now say: "How would you explain this world to this person?"

F. VACATION PACKING

Materials: easel; paper; felt marker

1. Tell the children: "If we went to the moon, we'd need to carry along certain things. What are they?"

2. List them on the easel. Read the list back and discuss the reason for including each item.

UNIT X

HOLIDAYS

This unit consists of *Important Ideas, Discussion Questions,* and *Activities* for the holidays of Columbus Day (October 12), Halloween (October 31), Thanksgiving (fourth Thursday in November), Chanukah (variable), Christmas (December 25), Martin Luther King's birthday (January 15), Abraham Lincoln's birthday (February 12), Valentine's Day (February 14), George Washington's birthday (February 22), Saint Patrick's Day (March 17), Easter (variable), Passover (variable), Mother's Day (second Sunday in May), and Father's Day (third Sunday in June).

Columbus Day

Important Ideas: Long ago, people were curious about the shape of the world. One of these people was an Italian sea captain named Christopher Columbus. He believed that the world was round, but most other people thought that it was flat. They thought that ships would fall off the edge of the world if they sailed too far. Many people also believed that great sea monsters would eat up the ships.

Christopher Columbus asked the king and queen of Spain for ships. He wanted to sail around the world to prove the world was round. The three ships they gave him were called the Niña, Pinta, and Santa María.

Columbus and his crew sailed from Europe, and when they finally arrived on land, they thought they had sailed all the way around the world to India. In fact, they had discovered a new land. Even though they called the people they met there "Indians," the new land later came to be called America.

Discussion Questions

1. Who has a father who hunts? What does he use for hunting?
2. How did the Indians hunt? Fish? Plant seeds?

3. How many people in the room have grandparents who came from another country? What country?
4. In what kind of ship did Columbus arrive in America? How do you think it looked?
5. What is the difference between Columbus's ships and the ships people ride in to cross the ocean today?
6. How else can people cross the ocean today?

A. FLOAT!

Materials: paper boat; plastic or ceramic plate; globe of world (or use large ball)

1. Draw a boat on a piece of paper and cut it out.
2. Show children what would happen if the boat sailed across a flat world (use a plate as the world): It would fall off the edge.
3. Then show them what would happen if the boat sailed around a curved world (use the globe).
4. Let the children examine a globe and find the continents and oceans—and their home town.

B. BOATS

Materials: colored construction paper; scissors; white paper; straws; paste; crayons; bulletin board

1. Have children cut rectangles for hulls and triangles for sails from construction paper.
2. Show them how to paste these shapes onto white paper to form a boat. Add straws to connect the sails to the hulls.
3. Tell children to color in the water around the boat and draw in portholes, anchors, and sailors.
4. Put the pictures on the bulletin board.

C. PRIMITIVE WAYS

Materials: pots of boiling water; cranberries, spinach leaves, beets; white cloth torn into pieces, approximately 8″ x 8″ (1 per child)

1. Explain that people used to make dyes for their clothes. The Indians, for example, made colored dyes from different plants. Then say: "We are going to do the same thing now."
2. Make dye solutions by boiling plants (cranberries, spinach leaves, beets, etc.) separately in pots of water. Allow the broth to cool.
3. Give children pieces of white cloth (preferably cotton, which takes the dyes better) to dip.
4. Let cloths dry.

Halloween

Important Ideas: Each and every year on the very last day of October it's Halloween, a night of ghosts and witches and pranks. We celebrate Halloween for many reasons. It is the end of the summer and the time when crops are finished and harvested. It is the day before All

Saints' Day, and in olden times it was called All Hallows' Eve. It is from that old name that we got the name "Halloween."

Some people believe that Halloween is the one day of the year when all the wicked spirits in the world can run free. The one condition is that they must return to their graves, or wherever they come from, before sunrise, because at sunrise the good spirits—the saints—once again take charge.

People today "trick-or-treat" on Halloween because in Ireland, 300 years ago, the poor people used to go to the rich people and beg for money to buy the things they needed for the feast day, All Saints' Day.

Discussion Questions

1. Are there really witches and ghosts?
2. What are harvests?
3. What is a jack-o'-lantern?
4. What food is harvested in the fall?
5. What is UNICEF, the United Nations International Children's Emergency Fund? What does it have to do with Halloween? Do you ever help?

D. PASTING PUMPKINS

Materials: oaktag; scissors; orange tissue or construction paper; glue; black construction paper

1. Cut out one very large pumpkin shape from oaktag.
2. Have the children cut or tear pieces of orange construction or tissue paper into 1- or 2-inch strips.
3. Glue strips all over the pumpkin.
4. Then add black cut out features of a face (eyes, brows, nose, mouth) and stem.
5. This entire process can be done by each child if you provide small pumpkin shapes for everyone.

E. BAG OF PUMPKINS

Materials: brown lunch bags (1 per child); newspaper; string; orange and green paint; paintbrushes; black construction paper; scissors; glue

1. Have children fill lunch bags with crumpled newspaper.
2. Then say: "Gather the bags at the top with a string and tie." Help and demonstrate as necessary.
3. Have them paint the pumpkin part of the bags orange and the top of the bags green for the stem.
4. Then tell children to cut out facial features from black construction paper and glue them on the bags.

F. WITCH'S MASK

Materials: paper plates (1 per child); egg cartons (½ carton per child); glue; felt markers; black construction paper; yarn; scissors

1. Hand out a paper plate to each child.
2. Have the children cut out two sections from an egg carton and glue them on the plates for eyes.
3. For the nose, ask them to cut out the pointed section that is between the egg cups.
4. Let them draw mouths with felt markers.
5. Have them cut out a black triangle for the hat.
6. Glue on the hat and add yarn to the sides for hair.

G. NAPKIN GHOST

Materials: white paper dinner napkin (1 per child); newspaper; string (5″ per child); black felt markers

1. Give each child a large white paper dinner napkin.
2. Have the children crumble a piece of newspaper into a ball and place the ball in the center of the napkin.
3. Then say: "Gather the napkin around the ball and tie it with the string." Help them tie, if necessary.
4. Give them felt markers to draw faces on the ghosts.

H. LANTERN

Materials: orange construction paper (1 sheet per child); pencil; scissors; stapler; white paper

1. Have each child fold a piece of orange construction paper in half, lengthwise.
2. You should then draw lines from the fold to within one inch of the other side. Children should cut slits into the paper along the lines you've drawn. Demonstrate, if necessary.

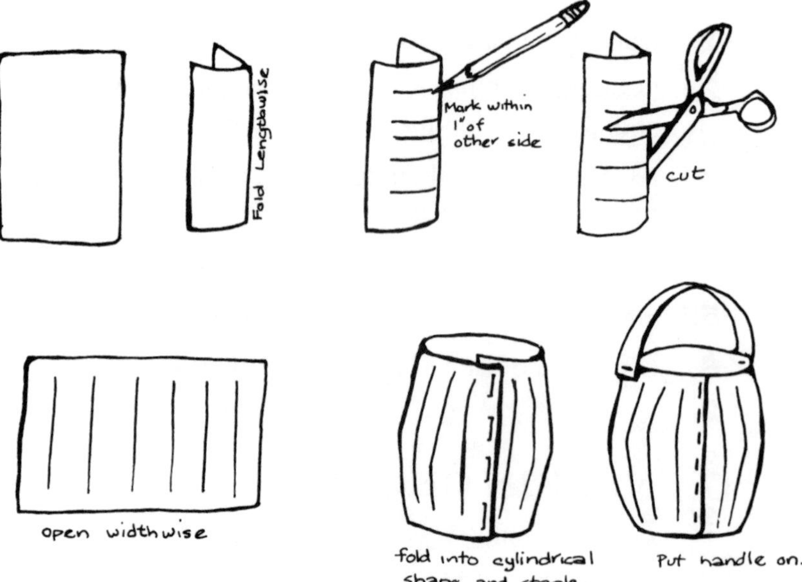

3. Then, tell children to open up the paper and roll it widthwise into a cylinder. Use staples to hold it together.

4. They can then add a strip of white paper for the handle.

Thanksgiving

Important Ideas: At one time, the Indians were the only people living in our country. They fished in the many rivers and hunted in the forests for animals, which they used for food and clothing. There were no stores in those days.

Later on, people came from across the ocean. Many of the early settlers came from England, because in England, they were not allowed to go to the church of their choice and pray as they pleased. These people were called Pilgrims. The first Pilgrims to arrive here sailed on a ship called the Mayflower. The sea was very rough and many of the Pilgrims became sick and died on the voyage. Everybody was happy to see land. They landed at Plymouth harbor, in what is now Massachusetts.

It was very cold. The Pilgrims hurried to build their homes before the winter set in. They did not know how to grow food, or how to fish or hunt, but the Indians showed them how. The Indians taught them how to put dead fish into the ground to fertilize the corn seeds that they planted. The Pilgrims were then able to grow a lot of corn. When it was ripe and ready to harvest, the Pilgrims and Indians got together and prepared a great celebration. They had a big feast to give thanks for all they had. The party lasted three days, and was the first Thanksgiving celebration.

Discussion Questions

1. Where do you spend Thanksgiving?
2. Who comes to your Thanksgiving dinner?
3. Who cooks Thanksgiving dinner and what do you eat?
4. What foods do you eat on Thanksgiving?

I. THANKFUL

Materials: easel; paper; crayons or felt markers

1. Ask the children what they are thankful for.

2. Put their answers on easel paper and let them draw pictures next to the answers or on their own sheets of paper.

J. NECKLACE

Materials: cut-up drinking straws; dyed macaroni; string

1. Tell children they are going to make Indian necklaces. Have available cut-up drinking straws, and dyed macaroni. (Dyed macaroni may be prepared by dipping pieces in a color mixture—half food coloring, half water—and allowing them to dry on paper towels overnight.)

2. Give children necklace-length string and show them how to string the objects to make a necklace. Knot it for them when they're done.

K. SHAKERS

Materials: paper plates (2 per child); beans; crayons; stapler, or needle and yarn

1. Have children make Indian Shakers by coloring the back sides of two paper plates.

2. Tell them to put beans on the white side of one plate and cover with the white side of the other plate.

Place dry beans in paper plate

staple another plate on top at rims.

3. Then, help them to either staple plates closed or stitch them.

4. Let children have a party with these favors.

L. HOUSES

Materials: Styrofoam cups (1 per child); scissors; felt markers or crayons

1. Give each child a Styrofoam cup.

2. Show them how to make a tepee of it by first cutting out a door at the rim of the cup, then decorating the cup with colors, and then finally standing the cup upside down.

M. CRANBERRY

Materials: blender; cranberries (1 quart); oranges (2); pineapple (½ cup crushed); sugar (2 cups); cups; spoons

1. Tell the class you are going to make cranberry relish together.

2. Mix cranberries and cut-up oranges in the blender (grind setting).

3. Then add sugar and pineapple.

4. Serve in cups.

N. GAMES

1. Tell children you are going to play games that Indian children used to play.
2. Start by running races, or having scavenger hunts.
3. When the games are over, encourage discussion about the Indians—what their lives were like years ago, what they're like today, etc.

Chanukah

Important Ideas: Chanukah is also called the Festival of Lights. It is celebrated by Jewish people in late November or December. The story of how this holiday came to be begins with a lamp. On one day in ancient times, a worker at a temple could find only one jar of lamp oil, and it was only enough to last for one day. But mysteriously—and miraculously—the oil kept the lamp lit not for one but for eight full days.

This is why Chanukah is celebrated for eight days, and why the menorah, or candleholder, is the symbol of Chanukah. On the first night, one candle is lit; on the second night, two candles are lit; on the third night, three candles, and so on. The first candle lit is the head candle from which all the other candles are lit.

Children get presents on this holiday.

Discussion Questions

1. How many candles do we light each day?
2. Why do you think children like this holiday?
3. What other holidays do we celebrate in November and December?

O. A BUBBLY BATH

Materials: small bottles with lids (1 per child); 1 tablespoon of white detergent; few drops of food coloring; 2 tablespoons of glycerine (from drug store); ½ cup of water; a few drops of toilet water, perfume, or cologne; yarn; glue; glitter

1. Help students mix all the ingredients together. (You may have to increase the amounts suggested, depending upon the size and number of jars you have.)
2. Pour this aromatic concoction into jars or bottles.
3. Tell children to decorate the bottles by gluing yarn around them and sprinkling with glitter.
4. Give as gifts.

P. PIN CUSHION

Materials: Styrofoam grocery trays (2 per pupil); scissors; glue; thick yarn; paint; paintbrushes

1. Have each child cut four identical triangles from Styrofoam grocery trays (used for meat and vegetables).

Cut 4 triangles from styrofoam trays

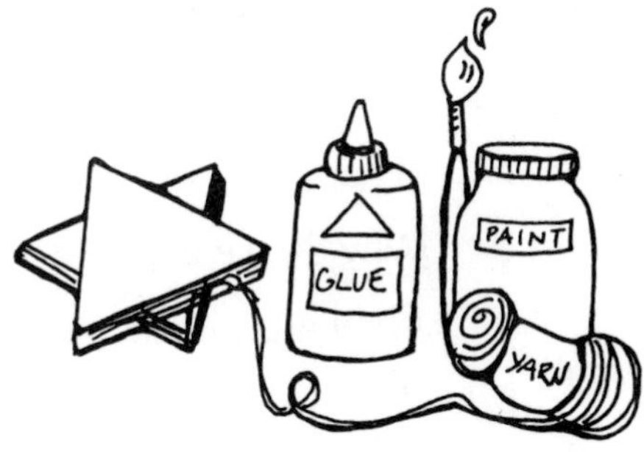

Glue triangles on top of each other to form 6point star. Cover sides with yarn and paint top.

2. Then tell them each to glue the triangles on top of each other to form a six-pointed star (Star of David).
3. Help them to glue yarn around the edges of their stars.
4. Let children paint the stars and then give them as Chanukah presents.

Christmas

Important Ideas: Christmas is a favorite holiday of many children. It is a time when many celebrate the birth of the baby Jesus. Many people believe Jesus was born long, long ago in a town called Bethlehem. It is said that from far away, three wise men who had been told of the baby came with gifts for the little one. They had followed the stars in the sky to find Jesus.

Today, many people exchange gifts at Christmastime to show they care about each other. Many families put up a Christmas tree in their homes and decorate it. Christmas is also the time of Santa Claus. He is believed to arrive on Christmas Eve by sleigh and reindeer and leave toys for boys and girls.

Discussion Questions

1. Why do we exchange gifts on this day?
2. What things do you think of at Christmas?
3. Why do we exchange cards with friends?
4. What are carols? Name some. Sing some.
5. What foods do we eat at Christmastime?
6. Do you see many lights at Christmas? Can you tell why?

Q. CHRISTMAS CARD

Materials: paper doily (1 per child); scissors; green or white construction paper; gold gray paint; box; pins

1. Hand out doilies and have each child cut out a bell or a Christmas tree (previously traced by you).
2. Tell children to pin the cut out shapes on the front of the pieces of white or green construction paper that they have folded to form cards.
3. Place the cards in a box. Help the children spray the front of the cards with gold paint.
4. After it dries, remove the doily and write a message on the card.
5. This process can also be used with cut out Stars of David or Chanukah menorahs.

R. WRAPPING PAPER

Materials: 3″ to 5″ sponge cutouts of Christmas trees; green paint; pie pan; white tissue paper

1. Have ready several Christmas trees of different sizes and shapes that have been cut from sponges.
2. Put green paint into a pie pan and have the children dip the sponges into the paint and then print the shapes on white tissue paper.
3. This also can be done with blue paint and Chanukah symbols.

S. CHRISTMAS TREE

Materials: large sheets of green construction paper (1 per child); empty thread spools; different colored paints; glue; glitter; scissors; stapler

1. Have each child cut out a large triangle from a full sheet of green construction paper.
2. Then, tell children to cut out a small rectangle to staple to the bottom of the triangle for the tree stem.
3. To decorate, have the children dip empty spools into different colored paints and print these on the tree.
4. After the trees are dry, let students add glue and the glitter.

T. CHRISTMAS WREATH

Materials: paper plates (1 per child); glue; scissors; pasta; spray paint; glitter; box (for paint activity); red bows

1. Cut a circle from the center of a paper plate. Do this for the children or help them do it for themselves.
2. Next, have the children glue different kinds of pasta all over the rim.
3. After the glue dries, spray the plates (in a box) with paint for the children.
4. Then, let children add glitter while the paint is still damp and a red bow on the top for hanging.

U. TREE ORNAMENTS

Materials: waxed paper; glue; glitter; red yarn

1. On a sheet of waxed paper, have each child make a squiggly design with glue.
2. Next, have them sprinkle the glitter onto the wet glue. Allow it to dry overnight.
3. Peel off the design from the waxed paper.
4. Attach a piece of red yarn for hanging the ornament on a tree.

V. CHAIN AND PENDANT GIFTS

Materials: plastic pill cups (1 per pupil); glitter, beads, or glass fish-tank pebbles; aluminum foil; cookie sheet; leather string; oven; nail

1. Hand out a small plastic pill cup to each child and have them fill the containers with glitter, beads, or pebbles.
2. Then, place filled cups on a foil-lined cookie sheet. Bake in a 450-degree oven until the cups melt down.
3. Immediately after you remove the items from the oven, use a nail to make a hole in each glob.
4. After cooling, let children thread pieces of leather string through the holes. Voilà—key chains!

W. CHRISTMAS ORNAMENTS

Materials: egg cartons; aluminum foil; large needle and wool string or yarn; scissors

1. Cut the cups from empty egg cartons.
2. Have children cover each cup with aluminum foil.
3. Help children to string wool through the top. Explain that they now have ornaments to hang on a tree.

X. PAPER WEIGHT

Materials: empty 8-ounce milk cartons (1 per child); plaster of paris; pine cones (1 per child); gold spray paint; glitter; box for spraying the paint

1. Give each child a small empty milk carton, which has the folded top removed. Pour into each a mixture of plaster of paris.

2. Before the plaster dries, have each child set a pine cone on the top. They should hold it in place until the plaster dries enough to hold it upright.
3. After twenty-four hours, remove the milk cartons.
4. Put each creation, one at a time, in a box and spray it with gold paint. Have children add glitter while the paint is wet.

Martin Luther King, Jr., Day

Important Ideas: Martin Luther King believed that all people should love one another, and should work together to make our country better.

In the past, we had many unfair laws. Some of these laws said that black children could not go to school with white children. The laws also said that black people could not sit in a bus or in a movie with white people. When black people and white people are not allowed to do things together freely, that is called segregation.

Martin Luther King's work helped to bring an end to segregation in this country. Today, children of all colors can be friends and go to school together.

Martin Luther King made many speeches in his life asking people to try to live in peace. He led people to Washington, D.C., where they marched together, black and white people, to say that they, too, believed that all people should be friends.

Unfortunately, Martin Luther King did not live to see the results of all his good work. He was killed by a man who did not understand the lessons that King was trying to teach us all.

Martin Luther King received a special prize for helping all people to live in peace. We honor him each year on January 15.

Discussion Questions

1. Do you think it is right for children of all different colors to go to school together?
2. Why do you think some people want to keep people of different colors apart?
3. Do you know what the word *prejudice* means?
4. Why do you think this man deserved to win a special award?

Y. IMAGINE ALL THE CHILDREN

Materials: paper and crayons for each child

1. Pass out paper and crayons to each child and ask them to draw a picture of one way that they, as children, could work together with other children to make the world a better place.
2. Pin up all the pictures on the board and encourage discussion about the different ideas: Would they work? How are they different from what adults do? Why don't we do them?

Lincoln's Birthday

Important Ideas: Abe Lincoln was born in an old log cabin in Illinois. He had to do a lot of chores when he was little because his mother had died when he was very young.

His father later married a woman named Sarah. She brought her belongings and lived with them and became Abe's stepmother. She was very kind to Abe and did his chores so he could go to school. She also brought some books when she moved in with the family. Lincoln read them all because he wanted to learn as much as he could.

Abe borrowed books from friends and one night he put a book between the logs of the cabin to keep it safe. It rained that night and the book got all wet. Abe worked hard to pay his friend back.

As Lincoln grew up, he was always kind to everyone—to animals and people. He was also very strong. When he was seven years old he chopped wood with an axe.

Later, Lincoln became President of the United States. We remember him as being one of our greatest Presidents. He led the country in a time of great trouble, for a terrible war broke out between the North and the South. Part of the war was fought over slaves, because many people at that time owned slaves. Slaves were people who had to work for others even if they did not want to. They were not paid for their work and were not free to leave if they wanted. They were often whipped if they did not obey or do their work. Lincoln, while he was President, worked hard to free the slaves.

He was shot to death while he was watching a play in a theater.

Lincoln's Birthday is February 12.

Discussion Questions:

1. What is a stepmother and where have you heard that word before?
2. How did young Abe get to school?
3. Can you name some other Presidents of the United States?
4. Who is President now?
5. What do you think the inside of a log cabin looked like?

Z. CABIN I

Materials: popsicle sticks (10–15 per child); construction paper; paste; felt marker

1. Have children paste ten to fifteen popsicle sticks onto construction paper to form the shape of a log cabin.
2. Then tell them to use a felt marker to make doors and windows.

AA. CABIN II

Materials: corrugated brown paper; scissors; construction paper; paste; crayons

1. Cut corrugated brown paper to the shape of a log cabin. Have children do the same. (If you like, you can also use the corrugated paper to make a three-dimensional model of a cabin for the children to look at.)
2. Tell the children to paste the log cabin shape onto a piece of construction paper. Show them how to do it so that the lines are horizontal like the logs of a log cabin.
3. Have the children add scenery (sky, trees, etc.) with crayons.

Valentine's Day

Important Ideas: This is a holiday where we make a special point to tell people we love them. Love is the special feeling you have for a friend, for mom, dad, brothers and sisters.

Today, we celebrate love on February 14th—Valentine's Day. People exchange cards, flowers, candy, and gifts with the people they like—family and friends. Many of these cards and gifts bear a red heart, which is known everywhere as the symbol for love.

Discussion Questions

1. What does love mean to you?
2. What is your favorite Valentine candy? Flower? Card?
3. How do you show your feelings for special people on other days of the year?
4. What does "Be My Valentine" really mean?
5. What is the color for Valentine's Day? Why?
6. What is the most unusual Valentine's Day gift you ever heard of?

BB. HEART NECKLACE

Materials: 2 cups flour; ⅔ cup salt; 1 to 1½ cups water; red food coloring; rolling pin; heart-shaped cookie cutter; yarn; oven; nail; mixing spoon; cookie sheet

1. Mix the salt and flour together. Add a few drops of red food coloring to the water. Add the water to the flour and salt batter a little at a time. Mix thoroughly.
2. Roll out the dough to about ¼-inch thick. Have children cut out heart shapes with the cookie cutter. They should then place shapes on a cookie sheet.
3. Bake the shapes at 300 degrees until they are hard. As soon as you take them out of the oven, put a nail through the top of each shape to make a hole.
4. After cooling, put a long piece of yarn or ribbon through the hole in each shape and tie it in a knot to make a necklace.

CC. HEART CENTERPIECE

Materials: popsicle sticks (1 per child); red construction paper (1 piece per child); white and pink clay; shoe box lid or any other box lid; green tissue paper; scissors; paste

1. Have children cut out hearts from construction paper.
2. Paste them onto popsicle sticks, and stand the sticks in lumps of clay.

3. Put these raised hearts inside a shoebox lid.
4. Crush green tissue paper around them to give the effect of grass.

Washington's Birthday

Important Ideas: George Washington was a great general in the Revolutionary War. He was our country's first president. He grew up on his father's large farm in Virginia. He liked to fish in the streams, climb trees, play with other children, and ride horses.

There is an old story that one day, while young George was playing, he chopped down one of his father's cherry trees. When his father came home and saw his beautiful cherry tree on the ground, he was very, very angry. He asked George, "Who chopped down my cherry tree?" George knew it was wrong to tell a lie, and told his father that he had done it. His father was proud of him for telling the truth.

Washington's Birthday is February 22.

Discussion Questions

1. What would you have said if you had chopped down that cherry tree? Why?
2. Have you ever told a lie? Tell us about it.
3. What is a President? What is a general?
4. Why is it sometimes difficult to tell the truth?

DD. GEORGE'S HAT

Materials: black construction paper; scissors; stapler

1. Have each child cut three pieces of construction paper to the same shape (see shape below).

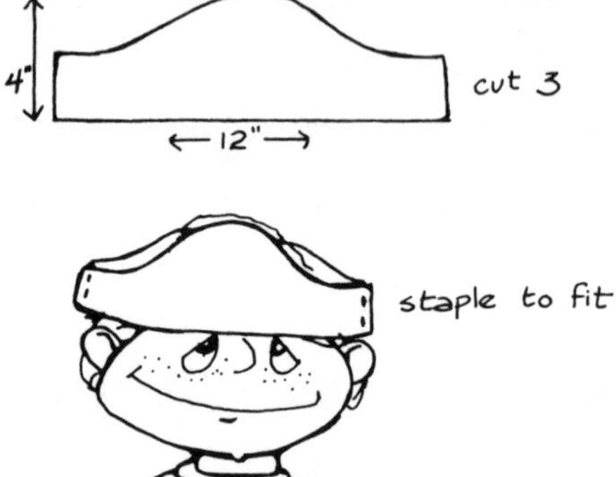

2. Next, help children staple the pieces together to make a tri-corner hat.

EE. GEORGE'S HATCHET

Materials: cardboard; scissors; aluminum foil; stapler

1. Have each child cut out a blade and handle from thin cardboard. Draw an outline of the shapes for them, if necessary.

2. Tell children to cover their blades with foil.

3. Help them to staple blade to handle to make a hatchet. Ask class: "What does this do?"

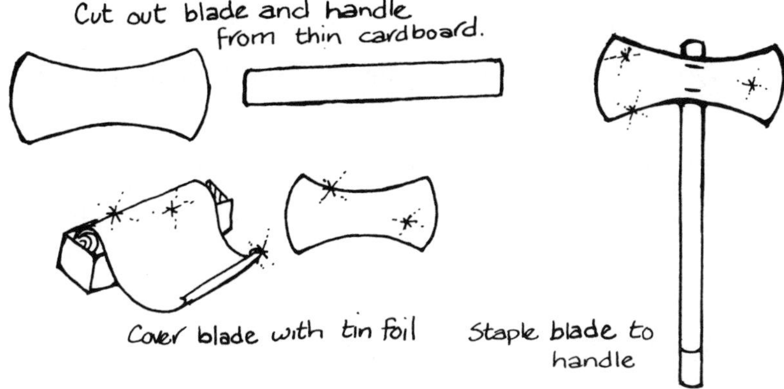

Saint Patrick's Day

Important Ideas: In Ireland, Saint Patrick is remembered during one day each year. He is Ireland's favorite saint. The Irish people feel he watches over and protects their country.

Saint Patrick's Day is often celebrated with big parades, both in Ireland and the United States.

The symbol of Saint Patrick is the shamrock. A shamrock is a kind of clover leaf. The saint's color is green. That is why you see green shamrocks everywhere on Saint Patrick's Day.

Discussion Questions

1. Have you seen a Saint Patrick's Day parade? When?

2. Who is Irish in this class?

3. Where is Ireland?

FF. SHAMROCK PATTERN

Materials: white and green construction paper; scissors; black felt marker; green crayons of different shades; stapler

1. Have each child cut out three hearts of equal size from white construction paper.
2. Overlap the hearts at the points of each to form a large shamrock. Add a green stem and staple the whole thing together.
3. Then, divide the shamrock into sections with a felt marker.
4. Have the youngsters fill in each section with different shades of green and with patterns.

GG. STUFFED LEPRECHAUN

Materials: paper bag; newspaper; heavy paper or cardboard; glue; yarn; scissors; string; black or red construction paper (for eyes, nose, and mouth); green construction paper (for shamrock)

1. Tell children to stuff a paper bag with crumpled newspaper.
2. Cut shoes from heavy paper or cardboard and glue them to the bottom of the bag.
3. Cut yarn and stick it into the top of the bag. Then, tie the top of the bag, but make certain the yarn (hair) is hanging out.
4. Make eyes, nose, and mouth from construction paper. Glue them on. Add a paper shamrock to the little guy's hair.

Easter

Important Ideas: Easter is celebrated in the spring. It is always on a Sunday. Usually families get together and have a big dinner.

Easter is celebrated as a time of new life and rebirth. To many, Easter is a time to celebrate Christ's rebirth. The day also marks the rebirth of flowers and leaves in the spring and the return of animals after the cold winter.

Children often color eggs on Easter and hunt for them. They also are often given chocolate bunnies and jelly beans. Easter is fun for boys and girls.

Discussion Questions

1. What day of the week is Easter always on? Why?
2. Do you think everyone celebrates Easter?
3. What do you do on Easter?

HH. BUNNY

Materials: beige file folders (1 per child); scissors; cotton balls; glue

1. Draw a bunny for each child on a beige file folder. Use the bunny from the next page as a model.
2. Have pupils cut out the bunny.
3. Next, have children cover their rabbits with cotton balls dipped in glue.

II. CHICKEN

Materials: yellow and orange construction paper (1 piece of each per student); scissors; paste; black felt marker

1. Have each student cut out a large yellow circle and two small orange triangles.
2. Next, have each child paste the triangles on the circle as illustrated, to form a chicken.
3. Tell the children to draw a black circle for the eye.
4. Put the chicks on the bulletin board.

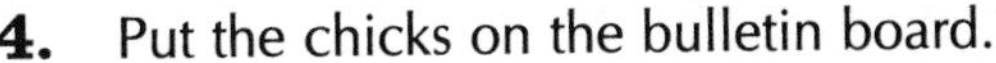

JJ. PAPER PLATE RABBIT

Materials: paper plate (1 per child); scissors; construction paper; stapler; pipe cleaners; glue; crayons

1. Use a paper plate for the head.
2. Have each child cut out two ears and a bow tie from construction paper, as shown.
3. Staple the ears to the top of each plate and the bow ties to the bottom.
4. Then, tell each child to draw a face and use pipe cleaners, cut in half and glued on, for whiskers.

KK. EASTER EGG BATIK!

Materials: white construction paper; scissors; crayons; thin green paint and paintbrushes

1. Have each student cut out a large Easter egg from white construction paper.
2. Next, tell children to decorate their egg with wax crayons.
3. Then, they should paint over the entire egg with thin green, or other colored, paint.
4. Put eggs on the bulletin board.

LL. EASTER CARD

Materials: lightweight plastic spoons (2 per child); 8½″ x 11″ construction paper (1 per child); felt markers; glue; ribbon

1. Fold an 8½″ x 11″ piece of construction paper in half.
2. Have children draw an oval face on their cards with eyes, eyebrows, nose, and mouth.
3. Next, cut two lightweight plastic spoons at the point where the bowl becomes the handle.
4. Glue the bowl sections of the spoons over the eyes.
5. Glue the spoon handles above the face for ears.
6. Add ribbon at the neck.

MM. EASTER BUNNY BAGS

Materials: brown lunch bags (1 per child); crayons; scissors

1. Cut a deep V into the bottom of a lunch bag (before it is opened). The V should almost reach the middle of the bag.
2. Have children draw in the bunny face on the bag.

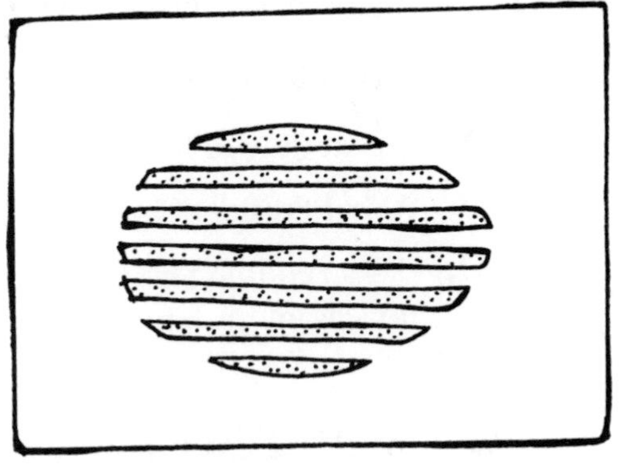

NN. CUT-PAPER EASTER EGGS

Materials: wallpaper sample book; paste; scissors; construction paper

1. Give each child a sheet of wallpaper (from sample book).
2. Have them cut an oval from the sheet.
3. Next, have them cut the oval into strips.
4. Let them glue the strips onto contrasting construction paper as shown.

Passover

Important Ideas: In the spring comes a celebration called Passover. It is celebrated by Jewish people to show their thanks for being freed from slavery.

The first and second nights of the holiday the entire family gets together and prays and eats a special meal that includes matzoh. Children are always included in this special celebration.

Discussion Questions

1. What do you think it is like to be a slave?
2. What President have you learned about who freed slaves?
3. If you couldn't eat bread, what would you use instead to take to school for lunch?

OO. MATZOH BAG

Materials: 9″ x 12″ pieces of blue and white felt (1 of each per child); pins; yarn; needle with large eye for yarn; scissors; glue; matzoh

1. Have each child fold a piece of blue felt in half and pin the two sides together. Leave the top open.

2. Have children sew the two sides together. Help them, if necessary.

3. Cut out two triangles from the white felt and glue them on top of each other to make a six-pointed star. Glue the star onto the bag.

4. Place a piece of matzoh inside for Passover.

Mother's Day

Important Ideas: Mothers, like fathers, play an important role in our lives. They love and care for children, and teach the children to love and care for other people. Many mothers have jobs in addition to helping to take care of their families. Children usually remember their mothers all their lives as being very special.

Sometimes mothers have to scold their children. But this is only because they want to teach the children to be the very best they can be.

If you haven't said it lately, tell you mother that you love her today . . . and everyday!

Discussion Questions

1. What makes a mother special to you?
2. What is your mom's favorite color?
3. How do you think a mother is different from a father?
4. What is a grandmother?
5. What do you do to thank your mom for her help?

PP. PIN CUSHION

Materials: empty spool of thread (1 per student); paint and paintbrushes; Styrofoam balls, 1″–2″ diameter (1 per student); knife (for teacher); scissors; calico material; clear drying glue

1. Have each youngster paint an empty spool.
2. Cut each Styrofoam ball in half. Have children glue half the ball on one end of spool and half on the other end.
3. Cut two calico circles large enough to cover each Styrofoam half.
4. Help children to glue circles over the Styrofoam.

QQ. MOTHER'S DAY CARD

Materials: 8½″ x 11″ construction paper; tempera paint; paintbrushes; peanut shells; red construction paper; glue; scissors; crayons

1. Have children fold their pieces of construction paper in half to make a card.
2. Tell them next to cut out a red circle to be the center of a flower and to glue it on the card.
3. Pass out peanut shells and have children paint them.
4. When the shells are dry, children can paste them around the red circle on the card to resemble flower petals.
5. Let children use crayons to draw stems and leaves after petals are in place.

RR. MOTHER'S DAY COLLAGE

Materials: magazines and catalogues; glue; scissors; construction paper

1. Have children make a collage about mothers. They should use pictures from magazines and catalogues that depict the things mothers do.

2. Tell children to paste the cuttings onto construction paper.

3. Then, have each child describe a special thing his mother does.

4. Send collages home to mothers.

SS. SPRAY A HAND

Materials: white tempera paint; water; atomizer bottle used for household cleaner; dark blue or black construction paper

1. Add enough water to the tempera paint so that it can spray easily. Pour the mixture into an atomizer.

2. Have each child place his hand on the construction paper. Step back and spray.

3. When hands are removed, their silhouettes will be visible on the paper.

4. Send these home to mother.

Father's Day

Important Ideas: Fathers are very important people. They help to teach children many things. Dads help their families in many ways. They often go out to work and also help take care of the family.

Many boys will one day grow up to be fathers and help take care of their families. Many girls will grow up and never forget how special their dads were to them when they were small.

There are many fun things we can do when we spend time with our dads.

Discussion Questions

1. Do you give your dad a present on this day?
2. What is the best thing about your dad?
3. How does your dad earn a living?
4. How do you show your father what you think of him?
5. What do you call your dad?

TT. A PENCIL HOLDER FOR DAD

Materials: clear plastic cups (2 per student and 1 for you); scissors; oaktag; markers and crayons; clear drying glue

1. The idea for this gift is that the child will draw a picture to be sealed between two plastic cups.
2. Cut out the bottom of one cup and then cut open the remaining plastic cylinder. Press that cylinder flat against a piece of oaktag and trace its outline. Cut out the traced shape and use it as a model to trace an outline on each student's piece of oaktag. This will ensure that the child's drawing will fit exactly within the cup.
3. Tell children to cut out the traced shapes on the oaktag.

4. Then, have each child draw and color a picture on the oaktag.

5. Show the child how to place the cutout inside one cup so that the design faces out. Then put some glue on the bottom of the second cup and place it firmly into the design cup.

Dad has a pencil holder!

UU. FIRECRACKER CARD

Materials: red construction paper (1 sheet per child); scissors; straws (1 per child); glue; felt marker

1. Draw the outline of a 6″ x 7″ shape on each child's piece of red construction paper.

2. Tell children to cut out their shapes and then fold them in half lengthwise.
3. Then have each child place a white straw within the fold and glue it in place. Help them with this, if necessary.
4. On the front of the card, write: "POP." Inside, write: "You are the greatest."

CHAPTER 4
Science Readiness

UNITS IN CHAPTER 4

Before the first grade, children traditionally are exposed to the basic language and quantitative skills (and occasionally to some social studies) that will serve them throughout their lives. But they are seldom encouraged to investigate those aspects of the physical world that are in the domains of science and technology.

This chapter is designed to arouse the innate curiosity that many four- and five-year-olds possess about the earth. The ideas are organized into nine units—one unit for each month of the school year. Simple biology is the topic of Units I, II, and VI. Beginning physics is the subject matter of Units V and VII. Geosciences are explored in Units III, IV, and VIII, and astronomy is the domain of Unit IX.

As in Chapter 3, each unit is divided into three distinct sections. The first, *Important Ideas,* offers a simple introduction to the subject of the unit and may be read to the class. The second, *Discussion Questions,* provides keys to the ideas that must be understood in the course of the unit. The third, *Activities,* is the means by which the children can investigate the concepts introduced each month.

In using the 114 activities of this part of the curriculum, you must be very aware of the extent of the students' vocabulary. In many cases it may be necessary for you to define terms.

The nature of this chapter has necessitated the inclusion of activities that occasionally require more time to complete than the activities in the first three chapters required. For example, activities involving plant or child growth cannot be adequately handled in an hour or an afternoon. Therefore, as a guide, there is an asterisk placed by those activities that need more than a day's time to complete.

UNIT I

LIVING THINGS

Important Ideas: All things are either *living* or *nonliving*. Animals and plants are living things. They can breathe and need air to stay alive.

The part of the air that animals need is called oxygen. Land animals take oxygen directly from the air into their lungs. In some animals, such as earthworms and salamanders, oxygen is taken in through tiny openings that are all over the body. Most water animals use gills to get oxygen through the water. But some animals who live in the water, such as seals and whales and dolphins, must come to the surface to breathe oxygen through the air—like land animals.

Both animals and plants need nutrients to grow. Most animals get their nutrients from eating plants or other animals. Plants absorb most of their nutrients and water from the soil. They also need light and air to grow. There are many kinds of plants. Plants take in air on the bottom of their leaves, where there are tiny holes that cannot be seen.

Discussion Questions

1. How can we tell if a thing is living or not living?
2. What is the difference between plants and animals?
3. Where do plants live?
4. What do animals need in order to live?
5. What do plants need in order to live?
6. Are there many kinds of animals? Name some.
7. Are there many kinds of plants? Name some.
8. What is the name of an animal with only two legs? (man, bird)
9. What is the name of an animal with no legs? (fish, snake)
10. What is the name of an animal with no fur? (frog)

11. What is the name of a plant that is green? (tree)
12. How small can living things be?
13. Do animals care for their young? Can you think of some animal that does not?
14. What can you, as a living thing, do? (run, walk, eat, sleep)
15. Are fish living things? Do they need air?
16. Why do birds go south in the winter? (to stay warm and find food)
17. Why do some animals sleep through the winter? (It is hard for them to find food when the ground is frozen.)
18. What do we call the birds' trip south? (migration)
19. What do we call it when animals sleep through cold months? (hibernation)

A. A BREATH

1. Ask each person to look at his own chest while you count to ten.
2. Ask the class: "Does your chest go in and out?"
3. Explain that the movement is called *breathing*. Breathing is taking air in and out.
4. Ask the children: "Do all living things breathe?"

B. ALIVE AND DEAD

Materials: rock; potted plants; small animal, such as a ladybug, worm, or gerbil

1. Set out a rock, a potted plant, and a small animal on a table or counter.

2. Ask the class: "What is the difference between these three items?"

3. Then, ask them: "What is the same?"

4. Ask the children: "Which ones are active? Why?"

C. WHICH HOME

Materials: picture book of animals; blackboard; chalk

1. Show the class a picture book that has different animals in it. Discuss the habitat of each species.

2. Then, make a list on the board: zoo animal, farm animal, pet, other. Ask the class to tell you in which category each animal in the book belongs.

*D. IT'S ROVER

Materials: pets from home

1. Tell the children that those with pets and parents that agree may bring their pets to class one day. But first, they must make an appointment for a day with you. Then, each child must describe his pet to the class before the day of the visit arrives.

2. Write down each child's description.

3. When the pet comes, ask the child to describe it again.

4. Then, compare the earlier description with the animal present.

*E. FEED BIRDS

Materials: store-bought bird feeder *or:* empty milk carton; string; tempera; liquid soap; paintbrush

1. Buy or build a bird feeder and place it outside by the classroom window. To build: Use an empty milk carton. Make an opening as shown at the bottom of the container and thread a string through the top, so that the feeder can be hung. The creation may be painted with tempera to which a few drops of liquid soap have been added.

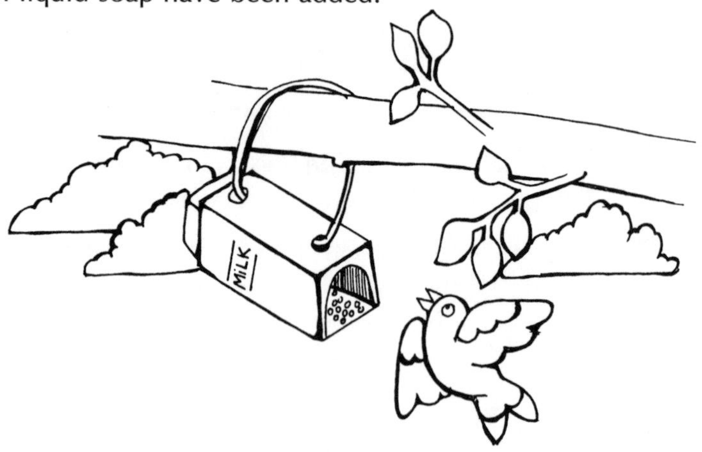

2. Have it be two children's task each day to observe the birds that come. Write down their observations, and periodically discuss the winged visitors with the class.

F. ANIMAL VOICES

1. Tell class members: "Close your eyes and listen."
2. Then, mimic the sound of an animal, such as a cow.
3. Ask them: "What animal makes that sound?"
4. Then move on to other animal sounds.

G. ART: ANIMALS AND PLANTS

Materials: drawing paper and crayons

1. Tell children to draw four kinds of living things: a very big animal, a very small animal, a very big plant, a very small plant.
2. Discuss the range of animals and plants drawn by different pupils.

H. NATURE TRAILS

Materials: blackboard and chalk

1. Tell the children they are going to take a walk around the school to see the different kinds of living things nearby.
2. After the walk, let the class help make a list of all that was seen. As they give names, put their answers on the board and ask: "Animal or plant?" Put the answer in the appropriate column.

I. PLANT NURSERY: A VISIT

1. Visit a local nursery or garden.
2. As you walk through, help the children learn the names of various species.
3. Point out what each plant needs to grow (water, sunlight, soil).

J. DOG HOUSE

1. Describe or show pictures of animal homes, such as a nest, a cave, a river.
2. After each, ask the children: "Who lives in this home?"

K. WHALES AND MICE

1. Tell the children: "Go through magazines and books at

home and find pictures of living things you can bring to class.''

2. Arrange the pictures around the room according to the size of the animal or plant pictured: e.g., one wall for very big animals, one for small animals, one for large plants, one for small plants.

L. THE QUICK, AND THE DEAD!

Materials: 20–30 index cards with pictures of living and nonliving things (one picture per card)

1. On cards, paste magazine pictures of living and nonliving things.

2. Tell the children: ''Sort these cards so that living things are in one pile, and nonliving things are in another pile.''

M. NATURE WALK

1. Take a walk with the class at least once during each season.

2. Ask the children to describe what they see and tell you how plants and animals have changed since the last season.

N. ANIMALS TOGETHER

Materials: paper roll; magazines, paste; scissors; crayons

1. Tell children: ''Cut pictures of different animals' homes out of these magazines.''

2. Have them paste the pictures on a paper roll to make a mural.

3. Then, ask them to draw, next to each home, the animal who lives there.

4. Then, ask them: ''Can you name any animals that make their homes from plants?'' Possible answers are birds (nests) and squirrels (tree trunks). Help the children out, if necessary.

UNIT II

OUR GROWING BODIES

Important Ideas: All living things grow, but different kinds of living things grow up to be very different in size from other living things. For example, a boy grows up to be a man and is bigger than a cat that has grown up from a kitten.

For growth, we need certain basic things such as food, water, light, air, and exercise. Each species of living thing, like people, needs certain kinds of foods to grow. Some foods are better than others, because some give more strength and more energy than others do. And we need strength and energy to work and play as well as to grow.

There are four different groups of food needed by all people: dairy products; meat, fish, and eggs; fruits and vegetables; and breads and cereal. Some foods (such as bread and fruit) come from plants and some (such as meat and eggs) come from animals. But all of it comes from living things. Thus, all living things depend upon each other for their lives.

Discussion Questions

1. Are we all the same size?
2. Were we all the same size when we were born?
3. Can you tell me the names of some things that grow?
4. Is it possible for us to see ourselves grow?
5. How do we know we are growing?
6. Why do we want to grow?
7. Are people the only things that grow large?
8. Do we all need food?
9. Do animals and plants need food?
10. What foods are especially good for us?

11. Do you like fruits? Name some.
12. Must we all eat exactly the same foods if we all wish to grow?
13. What are some other things we need in addition to food if we wish to grow?
14. How many meals do you eat a day?
15. Why should you eat a good breakfast in the morning?

*A. BIGGER

Materials: tape measure; paper (5′ x 1′); scale

1. With a tape measure, help each youngster measure his height.
2. Mark the height with the student's name on a piece of paper taped on the wall. Do this for each child.
3. Next, weigh each child. Put the weight next to the height on the chart. (Have children find out from parents how much they weighed at birth.)
4. Repeat this activity at the end of the year and point out how everyone has grown.

B. STAGES

Materials: magazine; roll of paper; scissors; paste

1. Have students cut out pictures of children of different ages from magazines.
2. Then, have everyone help paste the pictures in order of ages on the roll of paper. Discuss the stages all children go through: e.g., baby, toddler, teenager, etc.

*C. PLANT LIFE

Materials: potted plant; ruler; colored felt pens

1. Stick a ruler into the soil next to a plant. Point out to the children how tall the plant is and mark the height on the ruler in red ink.
2. Every month, mark the ruler again, in different colors, to show the children how fast the plant is growing.

D. MARKET FOOD

1. Visit a local supermarket.
2. As you walk through the market, point out foods from the four food groups. Also, point out the kinds of food in the grocery that different animals need.

E. PETS

1. Ask the children: "Who has a pet?"
2. Of those who answer, ask each to tell about his pet and to explain what is done to care for and feed the pet.

F. FOOD

Materials: bulletin board; signs for each of the 4 food groups; magazines; scissors; tacks

1. Make signs for the board: "Dairy Products"; "Meat, Fish, Eggs"; "Fruits, Vegetables"; "Breads, Cereals."
2. Tell the youngsters: "Sort through these magazines and find pictures of food that go under each of these signs. Place your pictures under the correct sign." Use pictures alongside signs if children cannot learn to recognize the words or read the signs.

*G. MEALS

1. Tell children: "Tomorrow, have your parents help you make a list of what you have for breakfast, lunch, and dinner. Then, the next day after that, we'll talk about your lists."
2. Discuss the value of the foods they have eaten and the four food groups.

*H. PARENTS

Materials: pen and paper to make lists

1. Plan a nutritious breakfast with the class. Write down the ingredients.
2. Send the list of ingredients home and ask the children to note, with parents' help, how many of these foods they eat each morning.

I. FAVORITES

Materials: blackboard and chalk

1. Ask students: "What are your favorite foods?"
2. Make a list on the board of the foods. After each child responds, ask: "Do these fit into one of the four food groups? Which one?"

J. HUNGRY

1. Just before lunch, say: "Do you feel like playing now?" or "Let's clean up the room."
2. Then ask: "How does being hungry affect the way you feel about play and work?"

K. WATER

Materials: orange or grapefruit; knife; celery; carrots; potatoes; grater; 2 dishes

1. Say to the class: "We're going to find out how much liquid is in some food."
2. Then squeeze an orange or grapefruit into one dish. Next, grate celery, carrots, and potatoes over another dish.
3. Be sure the children can see the difference. Explain to them that the liquid they see is mostly water.
4. Ask: "Do you think people have water in them?" Explain that most of a person's body is made up of water.

L. ANIMALS

Materials: blackboard and chalk

1. Tell children: "I'm going to go around the room and ask each person to name a different animal." Put responses on the board.
2. Then point to one of the animals listed on the board, read the name out loud, and ask: "Now, what does this creature eat?" List the foods by the animal's name on the board.

M. SNACKS AND THINGS

Materials: carrot and celery sticks; apple slices; fruit wedges; and other snacks of this kind

1. Plan a snack tasting party that includes only low-calorie, high-bulk items.
2. As children eat the items, ask: "What other animals eat these things? What food groups are these items from? Why are they good for us? Do you like these things?"

UNIT III

WEATHER

Important Ideas: Every kind of weather in the world is made by the sun. Whenever the sun shines straight down against the earth, the earth grows warm. Sometimes, the sun's light slants across the earth. The earth is colder then and the weather is colder. Sometimes, the weather is gray and cloudy. Sometimes it rains, or snows, or is warm or cold, wet or dry, bright or gray.

On a rainy day, the rain falls from clouds. One raindrop is made up of millions of small droplets. Rain, like all precipitation that falls on the earth, is water. The colder the air, the colder the water. For example, snow cannot come on a warm day. A snowy day must be cold.

Each flake of snow that falls has even less water than a drop of rain. Snowflakes weigh hardly anything, but since they are heavier than air they fall to the ground. When snow is hard, it is called sleet.

We choose the kinds of clothes we wear according to the weather. When it is cold, we need clothes that warm us. When something wet is falling from the sky, we need clothes that keep us dry. When it is hot, we need clothes that let us stay cool.

Discussion Questions

1. How can you tell when the wind is blowing?
2. Do you like wind in the summer? Why?
3. Do you like wind in the winter? Why?
4. Does air take up space? How can you tell?
5. What are different ways you use air? (for a sailboat, tires, balloons, swimming, inflatable toys)

A. WEATHER DAYS

Materials: magazines and scissors

1. Have children cut pictures from magazines that show all kinds of weather: snowy, sunny, rainy, etc.
2. Then discuss the kind of day the pictures show.

B. TURN, TURN

Materials: blackboard and chalk

1. Discuss the seasons.
2. Then, ask children to tell you changes that appear in each season—e.g., flowers, leaf coloring, snow, rain, etc. Write the answers on the board under the appropriate season.

C. HOLIDAY TIME

Materials: pictures that symbolize holidays (witch, Santa Claus, turkey, hatchet, etc.)

1. Show the class a picture that represents a holiday (e.g., a witch).
2. Then ask them: "What holiday does this picture go with?" And, "What kind of weather do we have during this holiday?"

D. SUNDIAL

Materials: stick (dowel)

1. Put a straight stick in the ground. Draw a circle around the stick.
2. Point out the stick's shadow several times on a sunny day.
3. Ask children: "Why do you think the shadow moves?"

E. WATER: HEAVIER THAN AIR

Materials: jar and fish tank or large container of water

1. Put a jar without a lid—bottom first—into a fish tank or large container full of water.
2. Tell the children to watch the bubbles to see how the air is going out of the jar and to watch how the water is coming into it.

F. AIR SPACE

Materials: drinking glass; crumpled paper; bowl of water

1. Crumple a piece of paper and put it into a glass.
2. Turn the glass upside down and push it into a bowl of water. Then, take it out.
3. Ask children: "Did the water touch the paper?" Explain that the air kept the water out because the air was trapped in the jar and couldn't get out. Air filled the space between the water and the top of the jar.
4. Let a class member try this procedure.

G. BLOW UP

Materials: balloon and jar

1. Blow up a balloon and try to stuff it in a jar.
2. Ask the class: "Why won't it go in?" Explain that the air is trapped inside.
3. Take the air out of the balloon and put the balloon in the jar.
4. Ask them: "Why does it go in now?"

H. OXYGEN

Materials: candles (2); matches; drinking glass

1. Light two candles. As they burn, explain to the class that it is air around the candles that keeps them burning. Air is what the fire "eats" to burn.

2. Cover one candle with a glass. Ask children: "Why did this candle burn out?" (Because it used up all its food: the air.)

I. PINWHEEL

Materials: construction paper; dowel (4′); tack

1. To make a pinwheel, first draw cut lines on a square sheet of paper. Use the illustration below for guidance. Once you have made four cuts almost, but not quite, to the center, fold

back the four corners indicated. Then use a tack in the center to hold the corners down and to attach the whole wheel to a dowel.

2. Take the wheel outside on a windy day. Ask the class: "What makes it move?"
3. Take the wheel inside and ask: "Why doesn't it move now?"
4. Explain that the air is not moving inside, so it cannot push the wheel.

J. EVAPORATION

Materials: chalk

1. Mark the outline of a puddle one morning with chalk. Then mark it at different intervals during the day.
2. Ask the children: "What makes it get smaller?"

*K. DRY

Materials: 2 jars of water (one with a lid) and felt marker

1. On the windowsill, place a jar of water. Mark the water level. Repeat each day.
2. Place another jar of water next to the first jar, but cap it with a very tight-fitting lid.
3. After a week, ask: "What happened to the water in the lidless jar?"
4. "Why didn't the water sink in the jar with a lid?"

*L. RAIN CHECK

Materials: glasses or jars; ruler; log chart for wall; felt marker

1. For a specific period of time, a week or a month, collect rain on rainy days in a glass.
2. At the end of the day, or the next morning, measure the rainfall.
3. Enter the figures in a log that is posted on the wall.
4. Let children see which days had the most rain, which the least, the longest dry period, the number of rainy days that month.

M. FREEZE

Materials: jar of water

1. On a freezing day, pour some water in a jar and place it outside.
2. After several hours, bring it in and let the children see what is happening to the water.
3. Leave the jar inside and let them observe what's happening.
4. Say to them: "Since most warm-blooded living things are largely water, they have to be protected once the temperature becomes freezing or they will freeze!" Then ask: "What would happen if the ice froze solid in the jar?" (The jar would break because ice takes up more space than water.)

N. STEAM

Materials: tea kettle; water; stove or hot plate

1. Boil water on a stove. Explain that the cloud of steam coming from the kettle is like a cloud in the sky.
2. Ask them: "Is the cloud from our breath in winter the same?" "How?"

*O. WEATHER CHART

Materials: easel; paper; felt marker

1. Using symbols for the different kinds of weather, you can make a chart to record the weather each day during a month.

2. At the end of that time, ask: "How many sunny days were there? How many cloudy days?" etc.

P. HARNESSING WIND

Materials: magazines; scissors; tacks; bulletin board

1. Give children magazines and tell them to cut out pictures of wind at work. Include: birds in flight, gliders, windmills, sailboats, kites, etc.

2. Put the pictures on the bulletin board. Caption: "Wind at Work."

UNIT IV

EARTH, MOON, SUN

Important Ideas: We live on the planet Earth. Earth is very large and round. But the sun is much larger even than Earth. The sun shines both on the moon and on Earth. When it shines on the moon, that light makes the moon shine and lets us see at nighttime. During the day, the sun makes our world so bright that it is hard for us to see the moon.

Life is possible for us on Earth because our planet is located at the right distance from the sun. If we were much closer to the sun, the sun's heat would be too hot for us. If we were farther away, there would not be enough heat. The sun gives Earth the right amount of light and heat needed for life as we know it.

Earth has an atmosphere of air. It supplies living things with oxygen so they can breathe. It also protects them, like a blanket, from the harmful rays of the sun.

Discussion Questions

1. Is the planet Earth big? How big do you think it is?
2. When do we feel warm?
3. What does the sky look like during the day?
4. What does the sky look like during the night?
5. How can you make a shadow?
6. Could you use your shadow to tell you when it is time for lunch? How?
7. What would happen if the sun did not shine for a long time?
8. How does the sun help us?
9. When can we see the moon?

A. SKIN

1. Take the youngsters outside on a bright, sunny day. Have them stand in the shade and then in the direct sunlight.
2. Ask them: "Is there any difference between the shade and the sunlight?"
3. "Why is there this difference?"
4. "Where would you rather be in winter? In the summer?"

B. SUN HEAT

Materials: 2 8-ounce glasses of water

1. Place one glass of water in direct sunlight, one glass in the shade.
2. After an hour, say to the children: "Stick your fingers in each glass." Then ask: "Which is warmer? Why?"

C. SHADOWS I

Materials: flashlight; paper; tape; crayons

1. Hold different objects in front of a flashlight after darkening the room.
2. Let children trace some of the shadows on a piece of paper taped to the wall.
3. Ask students: "Do shadows look like the objects that cast them? Why?"
4. Ask them: "Could there be shadows in space?" (Yes, because light can travel without air, unlike sound.)

D. SHADOW TAG

1. Take children out on a sunny day.

2. Tell them that they are going to play shadow tag. Explain to them: "The person who is *it* tries to step on someone else's shadow. If he does, then the person whose shadow was stepped on becomes *it*." Play the game.

E. DISTANCE

Materials: blackboard and chalk

1. Tell the class: "Go across the room from the blackboard. Now look at the circle I've made on the board."

2. Then say: "Come close enough to touch the circle. How did the circle change when you moved closer and closer to it?"

F. SHADOWS II

Materials: round objects (balls, grapefruit, etc.) and a projector or flashlight

1. Make a collection of round objects.

2. Darken the room. Shine light on the objects. Ask the children: "What happens to the shape of round objects in their shadows?"

G. BROTHER SUN, SISTER . . .

Materials: 4–8 sheets of paper; stapler; magazines; scissors; paste

1. Make a booklet by stapling together four to eight sheets of bond paper.

2. Give magazines to the children and say: "Cut out pictures of the sun and moon. Then, we will paste them in this book."

H. SHADOW GAME

1. Take the children outside.

2. Tell the children: "I will say something and you try to do it. First, stand with your shadow in front of you. Behind you. Touch your shadow. Shake hands with the shadow."

I. WIND FORCE

Materials: paper or Ping-Pong ball

1. Tell the children to blow on things such as crumpled paper or a Ping-Pong ball or a leaf.

2. Then say: "Could you blow it away from you? Toward you? Why?" Then point out that things tend to move away from the wind.

J. DAYLIGHT

Materials: masking tape

1. Place a strip of masking tape on the edge of a ray of sunlight falling on the room's floor.

2. Have the children observe it in ten minutes, in thirty minutes, in three hours. Ask them why there is movement.

K. DAY/NIGHT FLASHLIGHT

Materials: globe (of the world) and flashlight

1. Show the children a globe. Hold a flashlight above it. Turn the globe.

2. Then say: "See how one side of the world is in light and one side is dark. This is why we have day and night—because the world turns around and our side is sometimes away from the light."

3. Discuss how "day" and "night" on the moon causes different shapes of the moon (new, full, half-moon).

UNIT V

LISTENING TO SOUNDS

Important Ideas: Sound is made by people, animals, and moving objects. Sounds travel in all directions. We hear sounds with our ears. They may be pleasant or unpleasant. They can warn us of danger or fill us with laughter.

All sounds are made in the same way: they are created when something moves through the air rapidly. If that something moves rapidly back and forth, we say it is vibrating. All sounds are vibrations.

Most sounds you hear travel through air because the air can carry vibrations. But sound can travel through many other things as well, such as wood or metal. The one thing it cannot travel through is outer space. Outer space has no air or anything else for sound to pass through. It is a wonder the way our world has provided a way for us to hear and speak. We need the air not only to breathe but also to carry our voices and the voices of our friends.

Discussion Questions

1. What are some sounds you hear often?
2. How do we hear?
3. What sounds do we hear every day?
4. What sounds do we hear only sometimes?
5. Why does a dog pick up his ears when he hears a noise?
6. Many jobs use certain sounds. What special sounds are used by policemen, firemen, truckers, ice cream men, etc.?
7. How do sounds differ?
8. What are some loud sounds? Soft sounds? Long sounds? Short sounds?
9. Why is it good that we can hear?

10. Why are false alarms about fire dangerous?

11. What sounds are outdoors?

12. What are some pleasant and unpleasant sounds?

13. What sounds do babies like to hear?

14. How can you make a sound louder? (You can cup your hands to your ears, make a cardboard cone "hearing aid," turn up the volume control on a radio or tape recorder, etc.)

A. LONG WIRE

Materials: 2 empty tin cans; string (approximately 12′ long); masking tape

1. Take two tin cans and punch a hole in the bottom of each. Put one end of a string through one hole and tie the end in a knot so it will not pass back through the hole in the can. Do the same with the other end of string and the other can. Tape the open end of the cans' rims to make the edges safe.

2. Tell two youngsters they are going to talk on the phone. Give each of them a can, stretch the string tight, and let one talk into the can while the other listens.

3. Ask them: "Why can you hear with this phone?"

4. Explain that talking into one can makes the bottom of the can vibrate. The vibrations move along the string and make the other can vibrate.

B. VIBRATIONS I

Materials: rubber band and box

1. Stretch a large rubber band over the middle of a box that is missing a top.

2. Explain to the students: "When the rubber band is not moving it does not make a sound."
3. Then tell one pupil to move the band by pulling it up with one finger and letting it drop.
4. Explain that when the rubber band is moving up and down or back and forth, it vibrates and thus makes noise.

C. VIBRATIONS II

Materials: yardstick and table

1. Place a yardstick so that half of it juts past a table's edge. Hold the end on the table.
2. Explain to class: "When it sits there, we hear no sound."
3. Have one student pluck the end of the stick past the table.
4. Ask the class: "Why does it make noise now?" (vibrations)
5. Have students make the vibrating end of the yardstick different lengths. What happens when it is plucked?

D. AIR

Materials: large bottle

1. Say to the class: "When this bottle is still, it is quiet because the air inside is not moving."
2. Ask one child to blow across the top of the bottle. Say to the class: "The air moved and that is the reason for the sound."

E. VIBRATIONS III

Materials: drum and sand

1. Hit a drum and listen to the sound.

2. Ask the pupils to feel the drum just after it is struck. Say: "Do you feel the vibration?" Then ask: "What makes the sound?" (Vibration does.)

3. Put sand on the drum. Hit the instrument.

4. Ask them: "Why does the sand move?" (The sand moves from the vibrations.)

F. NOISE!

Materials: objects gathered from around the classroom

1. Make a class collection of small objects.

2. Have each student take an object and in some way make a sound with it. For example: rattle things in a box, rub together two pieces of sandpaper, shake seeds in a bottle, pull a finger along the teeth of a comb.

G. POTS CLATTER

Materials: 4 clay flowerpots of different sizes; 4 different lengths of rope, ranging from 1 to 2 feet long; dowel; ruler

1. Hang clay flowerpots of different sizes upside down from a dowel by using different lengths of rope (see drawing below). The four pots should not touch each other. They should hang

freely at different heights. Be sure the dowel is positioned so that the pots do not hit against the wall.

2. Tell the children to listen carefully as you strike the pots, one at a time, with a ruler.

3. Ask students to describe the sounds made. "Why are they different?"

H. PLACE AND SEASON

Materials: tape player; tapes of sounds from different places and seasons

1. Use a tape recorder and play back sounds from different places (farm, city, camp, and so on) and seasons (summer, winter, etc.).

2. Ask the children to identify each sound.

I. DANGER

Materials: easel; paper; felt marker

1. Ask children: "What are some sounds that warn of danger?"

2. Make a list of these on the easel paper (police and fire sirens; car horn; bike whistle, etc.).

J. CLASS VIBRATIONS

Materials: tape player/recorder and blank tape

1. Record various sounds from the classroom at different times of the day (lunch, story time, etc.).

2. Play them back and ask different youngsters when the sound occurred (snack time, etc.).

K. QUIET

Materials: blackboard and chalk

1. Ask pupils to be quiet for 30 seconds and listen to the sounds around them.

2. Open a door to the corridor and, if weather permits, a window to the outdoors to let in more sounds.

3. Ask what they hear and list the answers on the board.

UNIT VI

WHAT MAKES PLANTS GROW

Important Ideas: Plants have roots and stems that grow from seeds. And on the stems grow leaves and flowers. The flowers sometimes give way to fruit. The fruit has the seeds for another whole plant.

A plant's roots, born from the seed, go into the soil to get water and food. They also hold the plant so that it will not fall down or blow away. A plant needs good soil to grow well.

Green plants need sunshine. Their leaves catch the sunshine and turn it into food for the plant.

Green plants also need air. The air goes into the plant through tiny openings in the leaves.

A seed has the materials and food in it needed to start a whole new plant. The materials and the food come from its parent. When the seed is put in the right environment—soil or water—it can grow roots, stems, and leaves and, most amazing of all, more flowers and seeds. The seeds make it possible for new plants to continue for all time.

Discussion Questions

1. What happens to plants when they don't have light and sunshine? Or water?
2. What are the names of some kinds of leaves that we eat? (lettuce, cabbage). Of roots that we eat? (beets, potatoes, radishes). What are the names of some different trees?
3. What are the differences between a rock and a seed?
4. Do roots in a plant grow up or down?
5. What kind of plant will we get from a grapefruit seed, a tomato seed, an apple seed?

*A. GROWTH

Materials: dish; cotton; seeds; water

1. Fill a dish with cotton. Wet some seeds, place them in the cotton, and then wet the cotton.

2. Keep the seeds wet by watering everyday.

3. Open up one of the seeds after 7 days, then after 11 more days, then again after 15 more days. Keep the other seeds wet.

4. Observe the number of parts you see when you open a seed. Name the parts.

B. TO PLANT

Materials: apple; grapefruit; knife; empty milk carton; soil

1. Look at the way apple seeds and grapefruit seeds are placed inside the fruit.

2. Take the seeds out. Plant them in shallow soil in an empty milk carton. Ask the class: "What do you think will happen?"

*C. LEAVES

Materials: sweet potato; 4 toothpicks; jar filled with water

1. Stick four toothpicks into the sides of a sweet potato at about the center of the potato.

2. Place half of the potato in water by letting the four toothpicks rest on the mouth of a jar.
3. Ask the class: "Can a plant grow from this?"
4. Keep records of when the first sprouts appear.
5. Water the plant as necessary (to keep the half below the toothpicks submerged).

*D THE PIT!

Materials: avocado pit; 4 toothpicks; jar; water; pot of soil

1. Stick toothpicks in the middle of an avocado pit.
2. Sit the toothpicks on the mouth of a jar of water. Half of the pit should be in the water.
3. After two or three weeks, ask the class to tell what is happening.
4. Put the pit in soil in a container and record growth by measuring height and counting the number of leaves for each date.

*E. ABSORPTION

Materials: 2 celery stalks with leaves; 2 jars; water; red and blue food colors

1. Put a celery stalk with leaves in a jar of water colored with red food color and a stalk in a jar colored with blue food color.
2. After a day, ask the class: "What happened to the celery?"

*F. PLANT ME

Materials: seeds; planter with soil; paper and marker to make chart

1. Lightly sow seeds into a flat container that has soil. Make sure children count the seeds before sowing.
2. Ask: "How many of these seeds do you think will come up?" Make a chart of their guesses.
3. Water the plants once a week or when the soil begins to dry out.
4. After two to four weeks, record the results.

*G. LIGHTLESS

Materials: 2 potted plants

1. Have ready two identical plants. Place one in a sunny spot and the other in a dark closet. Water both regularly.
2. After a week, present both plants and ask the children to draw conclusions.

*H. UNKNOWN

Materials: pet seeds (feed) and planter with soil

1. Examine hamster or bird seeds and other feed seeds that are easily available.
2. Plant the seeds and see what, if anything, happens.

I. ART

Materials: seeds (variety); posterboard; glue; pen or felt marker

1. Have children bring many different seeds to class.
2. Tell them to make a collage using seeds and glue.
3. Label the kinds of seeds.

*J. TIGHT AND LOOSE

Materials: 2 trays of soil and seeds

1. Plant two trays of seeds. In one, plant seeds close together; in the other, plant them well apart.
2. Watch what happens. Make sure the trays are next to each other and get the same amount of water and light.

*K. SPROUT DAYS

Materials: cotton; dish; bean seeds

1. Place a bean seed in wet cotton. Keep it wet over several days.
2. As the seed sprouts, measure its growth over several days.

L. TREES AND FLOWERS

1. Walk outside of the building in spring.
2. Compare different trees and flowering plants. Observe likenesses and differences.

UNIT VII

MAGNETS

Important Ideas: Magnetism is a force. You cannot see magnetism, but you can see what magnets do. A magnet will pull some objects but will not pull other objects. Objects that can be pulled by a magnet are called *magnetic*. Most magnetic objects have iron or steel in them.

Magnets have strong and weak parts within them. The strongest parts have more force, or ability, than weak parts to draw magnetic objects. The stronger parts are called *poles*. All magnets have two poles which are said to be *positive* or *negative*. Different poles of two magnets pull each other together. The same poles push each other away. A compass uses a magnet as a pointer.

Discussion Questions

1. How many poles does a magnet have?
2. Is a penny a magnet?
3. How would you use a compass to find your way?
4. What kinds of things does a magnet pull?
5. Which things in your room are made of iron or steel?
6. Do all magnets have the same shape? Do they all work alike?
7. What happens when you bring two magnets near each other?
8. What would happen if you put a compass needle near a magnet?
9. How can you prove that the earth acts as a magnet? (It has two magnetic poles.)
10. What can you use a compass for?

A. NORTH AND SOUTH

Materials: bar magnets (1 per youngster) and blue and red felt markers

1. Tell the class: "Look at your bar magnet. One side has an *N* on it, the other side an *S*."

2. Mark the *S* side red and the *N* side blue.

3. Now, say to the class: "Put two blue sides next to each other. What happened?" Explain that like poles in a magnet repel each other.

4. Then say: "Put the two red sides next to each other. See?"

5. Now say: "Put a red and a blue side together. What happened?"

6. Explain that opposite poles attract.

B. MAGNETIC

Materials: variety of small items (some of metal, some wooden, some cloth); 2 shoe boxes; horseshoe magnet

1. Put several items such as buttons, pennies, screws, tinker toys, nails, and sticks on the floor. Next to these objects place two boxes, one labeled *Yes,* one labeled *No.*

2. Tell the class: "Try to pick up each of these items with the horseshoe magnet. If you can pick it up, put it in the *Yes* box. If you cannot, put it in the *No* box. Go to it."

C. PULL THROUGH PLASTIC?

Materials: 2 bar magnets; plastic cup; plywood; copper plate; cardboard; cup of water

1. Put one magnet in a plastic cup. Place the cup on the table. Put another magnet on the table.

2. Say to the child: "Slide the cup toward the magnet." Next, discuss what happens. Ask if a magnet can pull through any material.
3. Then put the magnets on either side of wood, then copper, then cardboard, and last water.
4. Ask if there was a difference in the attraction possible with these materials.

D. WHAT CAN YOU PULL?

Materials: magnet; cotton; iron nail; aluminum rivet; steel nut; brass washer; steel screw; rock; rubber eraser

1. Place cotton, an iron nail, aluminum rivet, steel nut, brass washer, steel screw, rock, and rubber eraser on a table. Say to the class: "Which items here do you think will go to the magnet?"
2. Point to each item and, after they respond, inch the magnet close to that object.

E. BROOM

Materials: magnet; ruler or dowel; string; pins

1. Make a magnetic broom by tying a magnet to a ruler or pointer. Spread some pins on the floor.
2. Have the children use the broom to pick them up.

F. STRONG!

Materials: strong magnet; metal paper clips; wooden table

1. Place some metal paper clips on a wood table.
2. Use a strong magnet under the table to move the clips. Say:

"Some magnets are so strong they can reach through thick rocks."

G. BEST SIDE

Materials: magnet and tacks

1. Spread some tacks on a table.
2. Tell class to find out which part of their magnet attracts the tacks most strongly.

H. NORTH

Materials: magnetic compasses (1 for every 2 or 3 pupils)

1. Hand out compasses and take the children outside.
2. Explain that the needle on the compass always points North. Show children how to use a compass and explain that compasses keep explorers from getting lost.

I. STRONGEST

Materials: 3 or 4 magnets of different strengths and metal paper clips

1. Place several magnets on the table. Place a paper clip under a piece of paper and try to pick it up with each magnet.
2. Try the same with five or ten clips. Which magnet is strongest?

J. MAKE ONE YOURSELF

Materials: magnet; nail; paper clips

1. Explain that if you have one magnet you can make another magnet.

2. To start, take the magnet you have and rub it over a nail. Use the same pole and move it in the same direction during each rubbing.

3. Show the magnetized nail to the class and ask: "How many paper clips can you pick up with this?"

K. COME TO ME

Materials: paper clips; glass jar; magnet

1. Place paper clips in a glass jar.

2. Tell the pupils: "Take the magnet and try to pull the clips out of the jar without touching the paper clips."

UNIT VIII

SAND, SOIL, AND STONE

Important Ideas: Sand is broken up bits of rock. Sand at the beach was made by water lifting rocks and pounding them against each other for thousands of years. The water acted like a hammer, pounding the many rocks into sand.

The earth is covered with different layers of soil. Soil is made of tiny pieces of broken rock, dead plants, and dead animals. Soil also contains air, water, and bacteria. There are all different kinds and colors of soil depending on what it is made up of.

Rocks are hard and nonliving things. They come in different sizes, colors, and shapes. Gravel and pebbles are small pieces of rock but not as small as sand. Some rocks feel rough and others feel smooth.

Discussion Questions

1. What can you think of that is made from rock?
2. Have you ever been to the mountains? What did you see there?
3. Where do pebbles and gravel come from?
4. If you could not see, how could you tell rocks from other things?
5. How do we know rocks are not living things?
6. Can we see different colors in some rocks?
7. How is the soil at the beach different from the soil at the farm?
8. What colors may soil be?
9. How does soil feel?
10. How long does it take wet soil to dry?
11. When soil has been dried, does the color change?
12. How can you make sand go through a funnel faster? Slower?

A. PEBBLE DISPLAY

Materials: rocks of different sizes, shapes, colors

1. Display pebbles or large rocks of various colors and shapes.
2. Tell the class: "Feel each rock." Discuss the differences—texture, shape, color, size.

*B. ROCK GROWTH

Materials: rock

1. Keep a rock in an obvious place in the classroom for a few days. When you first set it out, tell the children to keep an eye on it and call their attention to it on each subsequent day.
2. After a few days, ask if they've seen any change. Then explain it takes a long time for rocks to change, sometimes as long as back to the time of the dinosaurs.

*C. BRING AND SORT

Materials: rocks (brought by pupils)

1. Ask children to bring in interesting rocks that they have found.
2. Ask where they were found and ask them to describe the rock.
3. Once there are many rocks collected, ask the students to sort them by size, shape, color, texture, etc.
4. Ask children why a "pet rock" is funny.

D. DIGS

1. If there is any excavation or new highway cut near the school, arrange if at all possible to take the children for a visit.

2. Look for rocks you can bring back and discuss in the classroom with students.

E. LOOK INSIDE ROCKS

Materials: rocks; cloth; hammer

1. Children are usually curious about what rocks look like inside. Take a handkerchief or heavier cloth, wrap the rock twice, and hit it sharply with a hammer. *Be very careful of flying pieces.*
2. Compare the worn surfaces with the new exposed surfaces.

F. ART WORK

Materials: drawing paper and crayons or finger paints

1. Give each child some drawing paper and crayons or paints.
2. Say to the children: "Draw some pictures of rocks. The pictures can show rocks of all sizes that sit among other things like trees, animals, houses, and so forth."

G. SOIL EXAMINATION

Materials: soil and paper

1. Bring soil to class and place it on a piece of paper.
2. Ask the class to examine its color and texture. Then ask: "Do you see any rocks?"
3. Have each child bring in soil and repeat the examination.
4. Compare soils brought to class.

*H. LAYERING EARTH

Materials: soil; gravel; sand; plastic shaker; tall drinking glass; water

1. Mix together equal parts of soil, gravel, and sand.
2. Shake vigorously with water.
3. Pour into a tall glass.
4. Repeat Steps 2 and 3 a few times daily for several days. The children will notice components separate into layers. This is what happens to an extent in a river or at the bottom of a lake.

I. ABSORB IT

Materials: jars of several different kinds of soil and water

1. Bring in several jars of soil.
2. Add an equal amount of water to each. Have the class note which soil takes the water best.

J. STRATA

1. Go outside and look for a deep hole—but not so deep that children can be hurt. If you can't find one, dig a hole a couple of feet deep.
2. Ask children to look on the sides of the hole for layers: "Is the soil different in each of the layers?" Take samples back to class.

K. GRAINS OF SAND AND EYES OF NEEDLES

Materials: several cone cups; scissors; sand

1. Take several cone-shaped cups and cut across the narrow end of the cone at different places on each cup.
2. Pour sand through each cup. Ask: "What does this tell us about the sand?" (very fine, wet, thick, lumpy, gravelly, etc.)

L. ALL WET

Materials: 2 equal piles of sand and 2 cups

1. Take two equal piles of sand and wet one pile.
2. Pack each pile into a cup. Ask children: "What is the difference between the piles of sand? Can you make a bigger pile of sand if it is wet or if it is dry?"

*M. BRICK WORK

Materials: mud or cement and sand; water

1. Try to make bricks of damp soil, damp sand, mud, or a mixture of wet clay and sand.
2. Let the creations dry in the sun over a few days. Then examine.

N. CLUMPY LUMPS

Materials: tempera paint; sand; bowl

1. Put sand and tempera paint into a bowl and mix.
2. Ask class: "What has happened to the sand?"

O. SAND CRAFT

Materials: dry sand (colored); glue; cardboard (1 per child)

1. Make a design with glue on a piece of cardboard.

2. Sprinkle the design with different colored sand.

P. SAND JAR

Materials: sand (various colors) and jar

1. Layer various colors of sand in a glass jar.

2. Ask the class: "Will the sand stay that way? Why or why not?"

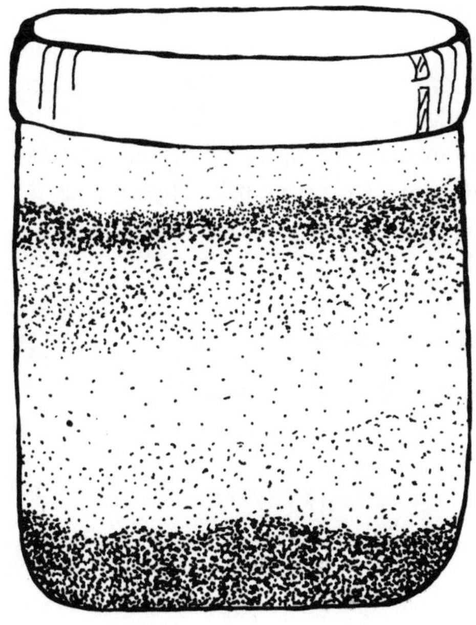

UNIT IX

THE MOON AND SPACE

Important Ideas: Conditions in space are not favorable for man to live unless he does certain things beforehand. Food and water must be carried in space for survival. Oxygen is necessary for breathing and for the release of energy in food. A space suit and spaceship are needed to protect people in space from lack of air pressure, extremes in temperature, and radiation.

A rocket can carry a person in a spaceship into space. From space, you can see the different parts of the Earth. The Earth looks round. To come back to Earth, the spaceship must slow down and then turn around. It may do so with the help of a small rocket.

The moon is called a satellite. A satellite travels around something. The moon travels around the Earth. Some man-made satellites carry radios that send messages back to Earth. They tell us things about space. Some satellites carry TV cameras. The TV cameras send pictures back to Earth.

Discussion Questions

1. What are satellites and why do we need them?
2. How is a person carried into space?
3. How can a person in space tell that the Earth is round?
4. How do space suits and spaceships help people to live in space?
5. What do you have to take with you to live in space?
6. How can you get into space?
7. What can you see when you get into space? (sun, moon, and stars shining in the dark; near Earth, you see land and water)
8. How can you come back from space? (Small rockets are fired against the direction the ship is going in to slow it down.)

A. SPACE

Materials: pictures of men in space (You can obtain pictures by writing to NASA: Audio Visual Branch, Public Information Division, Code LFD–10, National Aeronautics and Space Administration, 400 Maryland Avenue, S.W., Washington, D.C. 20546.)

1. Have children bring in pictures of men in space or provide them yourself from NASA.
2. Examine the pictures and discuss the equipment carried by the men.

B. CLASSROOM JET

Materials: balloon

1. Blow up a balloon to its normal size.
2. Let the neck of the balloon go so it "flies" around the room.
3. Explain that the push of air coming from the balloon is like the hot gases from a jet or a rocket that push a plane or rocket forward.

C. SUN RAY

Materials: chart paper; felt marker or crayon

1. Ask the class: "How do we protect ourselves against the sun?" (umbrellas, glasses, lotions, etc.)
2. Make a chart of answers using pictures as well as words.

D. HUMAN REQUIREMENTS

1. Ask the class: "Have you ever gone on a hike and taken a canteen of water? Why did you take the canteen?"

2. Then ask: "Why do you think the astronauts take along water?" "What other things do you think they'd have to take along?"

E. SPACE WARDROBE

Materials: picture of astronaut and a balloon

1. Tell children to look at the suit and helmet in a picture of an astronaut.
2. Ask: "What would happen if there was a break in the space suit?"
3. To show what would occur, let the air seep gently out of a blown-up balloon.
4. Explain that the suit holds oxygen, and without that oxygen the astronaut could not breathe. The suit is a safeguard against leaks in the aircraft.

F. SPACE TRAVEL

Materials: easel; paper; felt marker; drawing paper for students; crayons; ball

1. Ask the children to bring in pictures of a spaceship, inside and out.
2. Ask the class: "What do you think it looks like inside a spaceship?" Write their answers on the easel. Discuss.
3. Have them draw pictures of the inside of a spaceship.
4. Tell the class: "There is no gravity in space. That's why a spacecraft is needed. Without a spacecraft the astronauts and all their equipment would be lost floating in space."
5. Then bounce a ball. Explain that the ball would not go anywhere when you drop it without gravity. It would simply

float. Ask if children have seen pictures of the astronauts floating in the ship or outside on its surface.

G. SPACE FOOD

1. Ask class: "How do astronauts take food into space?"
2. Explain that it must be packaged (packets for food, tubes for liquids) for travel in space.
3. Ask what would happen if they tried to eat cereal and drink milk in space the way we do on Earth.
4. Explain that the food would float because there's no gravity to pull it down as there is on Earth.

H. SPACESHIP

Materials: construction paper; scissors; tape; paper-towel tube; glue; aluminum foil; string or thread; tack

1. Make a model rocket. First take a circle made of construction paper. Cut it halfway through. Fold it over and tape the fold to form a cone. (See also, Chapter 3, Unit IX, Activity D.)
2. Glue the cone to the top of the empty paper-towel tube.
3. Cover the whole thing with foil.
4. Hang it from the ceiling with string or thread and a tack.

I. SPACE

Materials: easel; paper; felt marker

1. Ask the children: "Why do you or don't you want to go into space?"
2. List pros and cons on the easel. Discuss the various responses.

J. THE JUMP

Materials: 4 strings (each 4 inches long); paper napkin; tape; plastic man (about 2 inches tall)

1. Make a parachute. Tape a string to each of the four corners of a paper napkin. Pull the strings together at the bottom and tie. Attach the small plastic man. Ask the class: "Why does it fall?"

2. Explain that *gravity* pulls it back to the floor. If there were no gravity the parachute would have no weight and would just float.

3. Explain that air in the atmosphere makes the parachute float slowly to the ground. If there were no atmosphere, it would fall straight down.

BIBLIOGRAPHY

Anderson, Edna A. *Families and Their Needs.* Morristown, NJ: Silver Burdett Company, 1969.

———. *Communities and Their Needs.* Morristown, NJ: Silver Burdett Company, 1966.

Barnard, Darrell J.; Stendler, Celia; Spock; Benjamin; and Moffitt, Mary W. *A Total Program in Science.* New York: Macmillan Publishing Company, 1962.

Bassler, Otto C.; Kolb, John R.; Craighead, Mary S.; and Gray, William L. *Succeeding in Mathematics.* Austin: Steck-Vaughn, 1976.

Benbrook, Joyce, and Foerster, Cecile. *Working with Numbers, Book I.* Austin: Steck-Vaughn, 1963.

Brandwein, Paul F. *Social Science Concept and Values Book: Blue, Green, Red.* New York: Harcourt, Brace, Jovanovich, 1975.

Caballero, Jane A. *Month by Month Activity Guide for the Primary Grades.* Atlanta: Humanics, Ltd., 1981.

Clymer, Theodore; Brown, Virginia; and Christensen, Bernice M. *Learning About Sounds and Letters.* Lexington, MA: Ginn and Company, 1970.

Craig, Gerald S., and Daniel, Etheleen. *Science for You.* Lexington, MA: Ginn and Company, 1965.

Croft, Doreen J., and Hess, Robert D. *An Activities Handbook for Teachers of Young Children.* Boston: Houghton Mifflin Company, 1975.

Davis, O.L., Jr., and Arnoff, M. *Seeing Near and Far.* New York: American Book Company, 1971.

Goldman, Ronald, and Lynch, Martha E. *Listening to the World.* Circle Pines, MN: American Guidance Service, 1980.

Herr, Selma E. *Learning Activities for Reading.* Dubuque, IA: William C. Brown Company, 1961.

Hoguet, Constance; Williams, Lynn; Sister Balthasare, C.S.F.N.; Abrahams, Carole; and Valentine, Sonia. *You and Your Family.* New York: Noble and Noble, 1974.

Jacobson, Willard J.; Lauby, Cecilia, J.; and Konicek, Richard D. *Searching in Science.* New York: American Book Company, 1968.

McAulay, John; Conte, A.E.; Burns, J.; and Skeels, D. *My Community and Other Communities.* New York: William H. Sadlier, Inc., 1971.

McCall, Edith; Rapparlie, Evelyn; and Stanek, Muriel. *Man and His Communities.* Chicago: Benefic Press, 1971.

McGrath, Edward J., Jr., and Krauss, Bob. *A Child's History of America.* Boston: Little, Brown and Company, 1976.

Martin, Mary Jane. *Lippincott Readiness Skills.* Philadelphia: J. B. Lippincott Company, 1974.

Matteoni, Louise; Lane, Wilson H.; Sucher, Floyd; and Yawkey, Thomas D. *Sundrops.* Oklahoma City: The Economy Company, 1978.

Nale, Nell; Haris, Thedore L.; Creekmore, Mildred; and Sucher, Floyd. *The Caterpillar Caper.* Oklahoma City: The Economy Company, 1978.

Navarra, John Gabriel, and Zafforoni, Joseph. *Today's Basic Science.* New York: Harper and Row, 1963.

Nichols, Eugene D.; Anderson, Paul A.; Dwight, Leslie A.; Flournoy, Francis; Hoffman, Sylvia A.; Kalin, Robert; Schluep, John; Simon, Leonard; Fennell, Francis. *Holt Mathematics.* New York: Holt, Rinehart and Winston, 1981.

Schneider, Herman, and Schneider, Nina. *Science for Work and Play I.* Boston: D. C. Heath and Company, 1961.

———. *Science for Work and Play K.* Boston: D. C. Heath and Company, 1968.

Smith, Carl B., and Wardhaugh, Ronald. *Series r: Macmillan Reading.* New York: Macmillan Publishing Company, 1975.

Stern, Catherine; Stern, Margaret B.; and Gould, Toni. *Stern Structural Arithmetic for Kindergarten.* Boston: Houghton Mifflin Company, 1966.

Suppes, Patrick; Phillips, Gussie; Carr, Ruth; and Kaplan, Jerome. *Random House Mathematics R Program.* New York: Random House, Inc., 1972.

Tannenbaum, Selma; Geise, Robert D.; and Pauline, Lawrence J. *People Who Made Our Country Great.* New York: Cambridge Book Company, 1970.

Thurber, Walter A., and Durkee, Mary C. *Exploring Science.* Boston: Allyn and Bacon, 1964.

Victor, J. *Math Prep Activity Book.* Danbury, CT: Grolier Educational Corp., 1976

Ware, Kay L. *Do You Know?* Austin: Steck-Vaughn, 1970.

———, and Hoffsen, Gertrude B. *Things Around You.* Austin: Steck-Vaughn, 1970.